The Archaeological Activities of James Douglas in Sussex between 1809 and 1819

Malcolm Lyne

Archaeopress Publishing Ltd
Gordon House
276 Banbury Road
Oxford OX2 7ED
www.archaeopress.com

ISBN 978 1 78491 648 0
ISBN 978 1 78491 649 7 (e-Pdf)

© Archaeopress and M Lyne 2017

All rights reserved. No part of this book may be reproduced, or transmitted, in any form or by any means, electronic, mechanical, photocopying or otherwise, without the prior written permission of the copyright owners.

Printed in England by Holywell Press, Oxford

This book is available direct from Archaeopress or from our website www.archaeopress.com

Contents

1. Introduction 1
2. The Excavations 5
   2.1. Long barrow and round barrow at Madehurst, West Sussex excavated on the 5th August 1809 5
   2.2. Barrows excavated at Rottingdean in 1812 8
   2.3. Three barrows on the Downs to the north-east of Preston, excavated on the 13th September 1814 10
   2.4. Four barrows at Balls Down (*Balsdean*) excavated on the 4th March 1815....11
   2.5. A barrow on Fore Hill on the Downs east of Preston excavated 19th June 1815 12
   2.6. Five bell barrows excavated on Balls Down 5th October 1815 14
   2.7. Barrow on Church Hill, Brighton excavated 21st October 1815...................16
   2.8. Two barrows at Black rock bottom excavated March 1816 20
   2.9. Barrows on Iford Down excavated in the spring of 1817 23
   2.10. Miscellaneous 25
3. Megaliths in the Brighton area 27
   3.1. The Goldstone at Hove 27
   3.2. The ?stone circle in Goldstone Bottom to the north of the Goldstone 28
   3.3. The barrow cemetery and stones north of St. Nicholas church, Brighton 29
4. Sussex Placename derivations and miscellania...37
5. Epilogue..57
Bibliography 59

i

List of Figures

Fig.1. Map showing the position of the long barrow on Rewell Hill, Arundel. Scale 1:25,000 7

Fig.2. Iron buckle and two Early Saxon pots from Saltdean barrows near Rottingdean. 9

Fig.3. Fragment from part-melted cu.alloy vessel from Saltdean barrows. 9

Fig.4. The Reverend Skinner's plan of the barrow cemetery excavated on the 4th March 1815. (c.) The British Library Board Add 33658 f.155. 13

Fig.5. James Douglas's drawing of an inhumation in one of the barrows excavated on the 4th March 1815. 15

Fig.6. James Douglas's plan of part of the Balsdean barrow cemetery. 17

Fig.7. The first part of James Douglas's account of the barrow excavation on Church Hill, Brighton with drawing of collared-urn. 18

Fig.8. The second part of the account with drawings of two Early Saxon annular brooches from secondary inhumation. 21

Fig.9. Two urns from Black Rock bottom. 22

Fig.10. Gold 'bracteate' from Iford Hill barrow. 24

Fig.11. Water colour from the common-place book showing excavation of a small Saxon barrow north-west of Brighton. 25

Fig.12. Sketch from the common-place book of two men, two women and a child attending barrow excavation at an unspecified location near Brighton. 26

Fig.13. Drawing of the Gold Stone at Hove from the common-place book. 27

Fig.14. Water colour of the Gold Stone from the common-place book. 28

Fig.15. Panoramic view of barrow cemetery and 'cromlech' on Church Hill made by Skinner looking north from church tower. (c.) The British Library Board Add 33649 f.151. 30

Fig.16. View of same barrows looking south-east towards church. (c.) The British Library Board Add 33649 f.145.. 31

Fig.17. View of same barrows and 'cromlech' looking west along coast towards Wick Hall, Hove with post mill in foreground. (c.) The British Library Board Add 33658 f.27. 32

Fig.18. Close up view by Skinner of 'cromlech' on Church Hill. (c.) The British Library Board Add 33658 f.30 33

Fig.19. Drawing from common-place book by James Douglas of large 'cromlech' stone viewed from south. 34

Fig.20. View of same stone from north.. 34

Fig.21. Drawing from common-place book of two men and two boys around large stone, which from its shape could be the largest one in the 'cromlech' on Church Hill... 35

Fig.22a. Etymons of place-names Cisbury and Chenck Bury (Chanctonbury)... 40

Fig.22b. Etymons of place-names Cisbury and Chenck Bury (Chanctonbury)... 41

Fig.23a. Etymons of Woolsenbury hill and Holingbury Camp 42

Fig.23b. Etymons of Woolsenbury hill and Holingbury Camp 43

Fig.24a. Etymons of Holingbury Camp (continued), Findon, Poynings, Pulborough, Billingshurst and Claydon. 44

Fig.24b. Etymons of Holingbury Camp (continued), Findon, Poynings, Pulborough, Billingshurst and Claydon. 45

Fig.25a. Etymons of Rotten or Rattendean, Oven dean, Odyor and Patcham 46

Fig.25b. Etymons of Rotten or Rattendean, Oven dean, Odyor and Patcham .. 47

Fig.26a. Etymons of Perchin near Devil's Dyke and Brighthelmstone. 48

Fig.26b. Etymons of Perchin near Devil's Dyke and Brighthelmstone. 49

Fig.27a. Etymons of Whitehawk hill near Brighthelmstone, Preston, Broil near Ringmeer, Blatchington, With-dean and Liddshill – Preston............ 50

Fig.27b. Etymons of Whitehawk hill near Brighthelmstone, Preston, Broil near Ringmeer, Blatchington, With-dean and Liddshill – Preston............ 51

Fig.28a. Etymons of Pang-dean, Tag down, North-horsh hill, Brach-pool-barn, various hills near Preston, Poynings, Lewes, Glyne, Radmil and Uckfield. 52

Fig.28b. Etymons of Pang-dean, Tag down, North-horsh hill, Brach-pool-barn, various hills near Preston, Poynings, Lewes, Glyne, Radmil and Uckfield. 53

Fig.29a. Etymons of Bedingham and Brighthelmstone. 54
Fig.29b. Etymons of Bedingham and Brighthelmstone. 55

Fig.30. Etymon of Selsey, with terse reference to a cromlech in a wood at Ardingly. 56

1. Introduction

In December 1987, the author was browsing through the shelves of a second-hand bookshop in Petersfield when he came upon a small, rather dilapidated note-book. On examination, it proved to contain various notes on barrow digging around Brighton between 1814 and 1816 with illustrations of finds, a section on the etymology of Sussex place-names, sketches and water colours of the Goldstone at Hove and other standing stones, as well as other miscellanea. There were no obvious indications of authorship but enquiry at the Sussex Archaeological Society offices in Lewes brought forward a suggestion by Miss Fiona Marsden that the Rev. James Douglas may have been the author: further researches confirmed this.

An excellent account of the life of James Douglas has already been published (Jessup 1976) and the brief biography which follows is based on this work.

Born in 1753 to an innkeeper at Hyde Park Corner, James Douglas entered the Austrian army as a cadet in Vienna after unsuccessfully acting as sales representative for his brother William's Manchester cotton mill in Italy. He took an active interest in antiquarian pursuits from an early age, making copious notes on antiquities seen during his time on the continent.

On his return to England in 1779, he obtained a commission as an ensign in the Independent Company at Sheerness in Kent. The construction of buildings and fortifications at Chatham Dockyards during this year had uncovered a Saxon burial ground and Roman structures: the chief engineer, Colonel Debbieg, supported Douglas's investigations of these discoveries and at least 86 burials had been excavated by 1782. Douglas was elected into the Society of Antiquaries in 1780 and was admitted to Holy Orders in 1783.

During these last decades of the 18th century, Douglas achieved a reputation as a polymath, delivering papers on archaeological matters to the Society of Antiquaries and a dissertation on the antiquity of the earth to the Royal Society in 1785. This latter paper was very daring for its day; postulating that the world was considerably older than the Biblical Flood. Indeed, Douglas's antiquarian writings, culminating in his *Nenia Britannica* published in 1793, are remarkably advanced in many respects.

He was one of the first antiquarians to be able to distinguish Saxon from Roman pottery and coined the word Samian to describe the glossy red fine table wares imported from Gaul: despite its inaccuracy, this term remains in use today. Douglas was also a pioneer in being able to distinguish primary and secondary burials in barrows: there is an example of this ability in the note book (p.21). He was also one of the first antiquaries to be aware of the principles of stratification and his section through the Saxon cemetery cut into by the sand pit at Ash in Kent (1793,25-6,35, Plate 9) is perhaps the earliest one in British archaeology.

Douglas's involvement with Sussex archaeology commences in 1799 when he was presented with the rectory of Middleton near Littlehampton, through the agency of the Earl of Egremont. This was a very poor living with the churchyard in the process of being eroded away by the sea. During his time here, Douglas started excavating at the Bignor Roman villa but the land owner stopped and replaced him with the much wealthier Samuel Lysons. Financial problems cast a long shadow over Douglas's life until he acquired the living at Preston near Brighton in 1812. During this period between 1799 and 1812, however, he established contacts with two great antiquarians of the day, Sir Richard Colt Hoare and William Cunnington, and exercised some influence over their methods in the field.

With the parsonage at Preston, Douglas was offered the chaplaincy of the troops at Brighton; a post which ensured him a constant supply of labourers for his barrow diggings from the ranks of the 10th Royal Hussars. He died at his vicarage at Preston in November 1819 and was followed by his wife six months later. His antiquities and papers passed into the hands of his daughter Mrs Tucker but were then left in the care of his artist friend Mr Prince-Hoare at Brighton. A manuscript list of items offered by Prince-Hoare to Sir Richard Colt Hoare survives in the Ashmolean Museum at Oxford. The last items on the list are 'a large box containing various Mss, among which is his folio Common Place Book, and another box containing various papers, letters etc, also a smaller parcel of Mss, chiefly dramatic'. At the bottom of the list is a note by Prince-Hoare stating that these last items had actually been purchased by him for £10 for the sake of sending a little money to Mrs Tucker. The antiquities were eventually purchased by the Ashmolean Museum but the papers were rejected and returned to Brighton.

I suspect that the folio Common Place Book referred to above is the present discovery, although it was thought by Jessup (1976) to be that of Heneage Finch, Fifth Earl of Winchelsea, known to have been in Douglas's possession. This Common Place book, together with Douglas's surviving correspondence with Sir Richard Colt Hoare, William Cunnington, the Reverend John Skinner of Camerton and a few other sources, enables us to reconstruct some of his archaeological activities in Sussex between 1809 and 1817.

2. The Excavations

2.1. Long barrow and round barrow at Madehurst, West Sussex excavated on the 5th August 1809

There are four surviving references to this excavation. The first is in a letter by James Douglas to William Cunnington dated 7th July 1809 and announces his discovery of a long barrow at *an almost inaccessible height* on the South Downs and *at a very considerable distance from any other barrow*. It is described as *overlooking a british road deeply excavated for its ascent to the hill*. Douglas announced his intention to open it (Wiltshire County Archives, Stourhead Archive 383.907).

The next letter to William Cunnington, dated the 11th August, gives a detailed account of the excavation, describing the barrow as situated on top of a very steep hill called Rundel, near Dale Park, the seat of Sir G. Thomas about four miles from Arundel. The ascent to the barrow is described as being by an ancient British road winding around the hill. A deep entrenchment crossed this road at right angles about 60 paces from the barrow and stopped at the steep hill slope. This entrenchment on which were large yew trees at least one thousand years old, is described as running in a line to the sea in the low grounds on the west side of Littlehampton. The view from the top of Rundel Hill is described as being most expansive, encompassing the Isle of Wight and the countryside around Chichester.

Douglas goes on to describe the finding of a skeleton at the broadest, south-south-westerly end of the 50 feet long barrow. The head was at the north-north-east end of the interment with the skull on its right side. The left femur was over the right one and the left radius over the breast. In the fill of the grave, about a foot above the feet were two pairs of large red deer antlers parallel with each other and about a foot apart with their root ends in the same direction. Douglas observed a yellow mould under the bones, which he thought was a thin sheeting of clay over the natural chalk.

The skeleton was estimated to be of a man 6 feet tall with the frontal bone of the skull having the unusual feature of being divided into two by a suture descending to the nasal bones. Douglas was of the opinion that the bones were those of a young man.

The letter finishes with Douglas saying that he still needed to finish the long barrow excavation and that he had opened a nearby round barrow on the same day with fragments of unbaked urn (Ibid.).

The third reference to this excavation is in a letter written by James Douglas to the Rev. John Skinner of Camerton on the 28th June 1816. This provides the additional information that the long barrow was near Madehurst and that the frontal bone of the skull was very narrow with the *bragmatis* extremely oblongated: the skull was thin. Douglas goes on to state that the two pairs of antlers over the feet emitted a most foetid gaseous effluvia when removed (BM AD MS 33665).

The final reference is much later in date and is in a note about a lecture given by a Mr Thomas King of Chichester (1845). This states that the barrow was of coarse gravel with only slight elevation and lacked side ditches: fragments of charred wood were found in the mound. There are, however, inconsistencies in this final reference which suggest that the lecturer was relying very much on hearsay. King states that the barrow was oval whereas Douglas says that it was wider at the south-south-west end. The accompanying illustration shows the skeleton laid on its back with one pair of antlers under its feet, whereas Douglas's contemporary account gives two pairs of antlers above the feet in the fill of the grave. The illustration is clearly unreliable.

Grinsell (1934,p.249} lists the long barrow as an oval round barrow at an uncertain place in the parish of Madehurst; basing his classification on Thomas King's somewhat unreliable account. The earlier description by Douglas does, however, suggest that we are dealing with a long barrow, albeit a rather small one. Rundel hill seems to be one and the same as Rewell hill, with the site of the barrow being now covered over by woodland. The Ancient British road described as winding round the hill is shown as an east-west ditch or hollow way on the 2 1/2" Ordnance Survey map running from SU97550875 to SU98000875. It then intersects with the northern end of a ditch running north to south as far as SU97920840: there are, however, no obvious indications of this ditch continuing as far south as the coast as Douglas stated. It would appear that the long barrow was situated at or near SU98050870 on the western end of the summit of Rewell hill as this is the only place in the area which would present the panoramic view described by Douglas (Fig.1).

2. The Excavations

Fig.1. Map showing the position of the long barrow on Rewell Hill, Arundel. Scale 1:25,000

More recently, the eminent Sussex archaeologists of the 1920s and 30s, Elliott and Cecil Curwen, discovered what they described as a 'circus' in Rewell Wood at a place which coincides with the position of the long barrow and comprises two curved banks of earth flanking a hollow (Curwen and Curwen 1920,28). This amphitheatre-like feature has been examined again more recently (McOmish and Hayden 2015) and is almost certainly the upcast from Douglas's total excavation of the long barrow.

2.2. Barrows excavated at Rottingdean in 1812

The sole surviving account of these excavations is in a letter by Douglas to Richard Colt-Hoare dated 25th June 1812. This is best quoted in full:

> *'I have been with a party, Col. 'Crips', the companion to Dr.Clarke the traveller and several other dilitante friends, exploring some barrows near Rotten dean. They began earlier than I could attend, on a large flat british barrow without system, excavating trenches from the circumference to the center; without attacking the primary. Skeletons were discovered, and about two urns; distant after deposits; of more posterior shapes than the higher british; though of the friable pottery. These with numerous other facts convince me that comburation and inhumation prevailed at a contemporary era. The center I broke into; but time did not allow of a satisfactory ransack. This I must defer to some other day. We also opened a group of the lower british small bell fashioned barrows: a few only; urns of a similar pottery and shape of the one I sent you; with the calcined bones, small iron buckles and fragments of a brass arferial vessel, melted in part by an ardent fire'.*

There is no report in the common-place book but an illustration of what appear to be the two pots and an iron buckle on one of the pages is entitled Salt Dean barrows near Ratten Dean (Fig.2). The pots are probably Early Saxon in date (c.450-650), with the first one being paralleled in form at Bishopstone (Bell 1977,Fig.101,5 and Fig.103,20) and the second at the Hassocks cemetery (Lyne 1994,Fig.13-122).

The following page in the common-place book has a painting of what is described as a 'Fragment of a brass vessel found in the barrow near the burnt bones' (Fig.3).

2. The Excavations

FIG.2. IRON BUCKLE AND TWO EARLY SAXON POTS FROM SALTDEAN BARROWS NEAR ROTTINGDEAN.

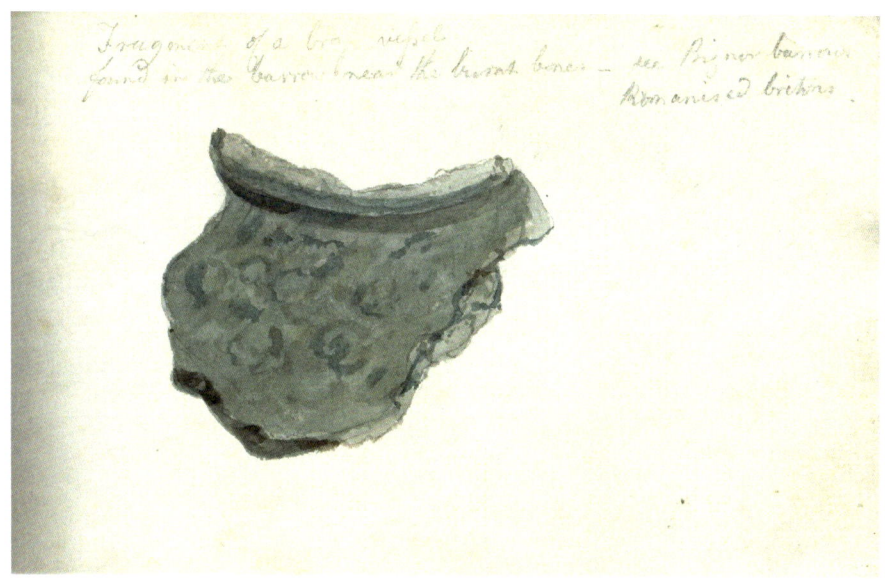

FIG.3. FRAGMENT FROM PART-MELTED CU.ALLOY VESSEL FROM SALTDEAN BARROWS.

2.3. Three barrows on the Downs to the north-east of Preston, excavated on the 13th September 1814

This is the first excavation recorded in the common-place book.

'Opened a barrow of the most ancient class which in the order of british sepulchres may with propriety be deemed Celtic – a term usually applied by the antiquary to the class of large barrows scattered over downs and waste lands; and distinct from the smaller class of the Campaniform barrows found in groupes, which contain skeletons only or barrows of the same shape and in groupes which contain small urns of baked earth and some with the marks of the lathe. Before the celtic barrow is described it is necessary to mark that the relics found in the skeleton barrows consist of iron spear heads, umbowes of shields, swords two feet 4 inches in length or 3 feet, knives and iron buckles. They are connected with the graves of men. Those relics in the graves of women or children consist of circular fibulae or long ones of this form (Here is inserted a drawing of a radiate-headed brooch) sometimes inlaid with garnets, of silver gilt or brass gilt – beads of amber, glass – broachs – crystal stones – glass vessels and various other interesting articles – pensile coins of Gaulish kings and of the lower Emperors, with other evident proofs that these barrows must class with a people interred after the departure of the Romans about the beginning of the 5th century.

The other class of small campaniform barrows in groupes, contain small urns with burnt bones, small brass and iron buckles, sometimes a small comb of ivory in a small urn by the side of the opiary urn – evidently a criterion of a woman's interment sometimes the remains of brass small vessels evidently melted by combustion. These urn burials may apply to the graves of the romanised Britons agricultural inhabitants of the neighbouring places.

The Celtic barrow was situated on the down to the north east of the village of Preston near Brighton; full north from the road which leads to Brighton about 2 hundred yards. Twelve feet in diameter coated with flint stones. The primary interment full in the center. The urn inverted over the ashes just under the sod with a few flint stones over it: rather let into a circular cist of the chalk, with a few bolter flints surrounding it. From fragments of the fistular bones, some evidence may be deduced from their texture and size, that they were the remains of a woman – and from some small rib bones and others, Mr Jenks surgeon to the 10th Royal Hussars who was present,

> *conceived they may have been those of a child; burned with the mother in the funeral pile and inclosed with her remains in the urn.*
> *Incontrovertible proof may be advanced to ascribe this order of urn burial to the earliest inhabitants of Britain viz. Nen Brit and Hoare's Ancient Wiltshire. The urn was about one foot in height and ¾ in diameter of unburnt clay – or clay indurated by the funeral fire, sufficiently so, to retain the burnt bones. Two more tumuli are at a small distance: the one to the south west has been opened – since opened and found undisturbed – a skeleton, iron knife and some other iron relics – the head to the west*

There is another account of this excavation in a letter written by Douglas to the Revd John Skinner on the 13th November 1815.

> '13th September 1814. I opened a British Barrow on the Downs above my village on the trackway to Hollingbury, a Belgic interment. Inverted urn over ashes, which appeared to have been the burnt remains of a woman and child by the fragments of the skulls and fistular bones – urn as usual of unbaked clay or sufficiently hardened by the funeral fire to receive the ashes: one foot in height ¾ breadth; coarse clay'.

There is no illustration of the urn in the notebook, so we cannot be sure what type it was. Nevertheless, we can infer a Bronze Age date for it. The description of the coins in the common-place book entry as being 'pensile' must allude to them being perforated for suspension on necklaces.

2.4. Four barrows at Balls Down (*Balsdean*) excavated on the 4th March 1815

There are records of this excavation in both Douglas's common-place book and in the Rev. John Skinner of Camerton's papers. Douglas's entry reads thus:

> 'Opened four barrows on Bel or Balls down-Baal in company with the Reverend Messrs Rice, Scholefield, Skinner and Maidwell. The group consists of seventeen – 7 I opened two years ago – found only a silver ring knife and small iron relics – the contents of two graves: the skeletons measuring five feet 6 or 7 inches – concluded women.

> *These graves are all of the lower order – containing skeletons. Two soldiers of the 18th Dragoons quartered at Rotten Dean on outpost duty in November 1814 opened two – one of the men having been my labourer conceiving I had been digging for treasure, clandestinely opened one of the largest – which contained female ornaments of some value.*
> *The four on the 4th March, only skeletons – the one out of the range and withisetaside the agger contained a skeleton near 6 feet in length. The head reclined on the left side, right arm over the left breast. One within the range near the centre of the groupe and opposite the large one opened by the soldiers – the skull reclined on the left side – right arm over the left breast. The teeth perfectly sound and extremely beautiful. The scull well preserved, orions and ?scave friable – under it some fine vegetable fibres something like hair; but apparently as if deposited originally under the head. The other two for want of time were not correctly or entirely opened. These barrows are of the same order as those of the Campaniform – see Nenia, and referable to the beginning of the fifth – to the latter end of the 7th centuries – lower british'.*

The Rev John Skinner's account of the excavation is somewhat terser and adds nothing new: it is, however, accompanied by a plan of the barrow cemetery (Fig.4, BM ADD CH 33649 p.155) with three of the excavated barrows indicated and a drawing of one of the skeletons on a page cut from the common-place book. The common-place book itself contains a drawing of the other skeleton by James Douglas (Fig.5).

The common-place book also includes a plan of the barrow cemetery showing the layout of eight of them (Fig.6). This plan is undated but the words 'silver ring and knife' written against one of the barrows suggest that it was drawn up when Douglas excavated the seven barrows two years before. There is no further information on this earlier dig.

2.5. A barrow on Fore Hill on the Downs east of Preston excavated 19th June 1815

There are two accounts of this excavation, both by Douglas. The first is in his common-place book:

> *'Opened a barrow on Fore hill on the down to the east of the village of Preston, distance ¾ of a mile. Skeleton deposited in a cist of the native*

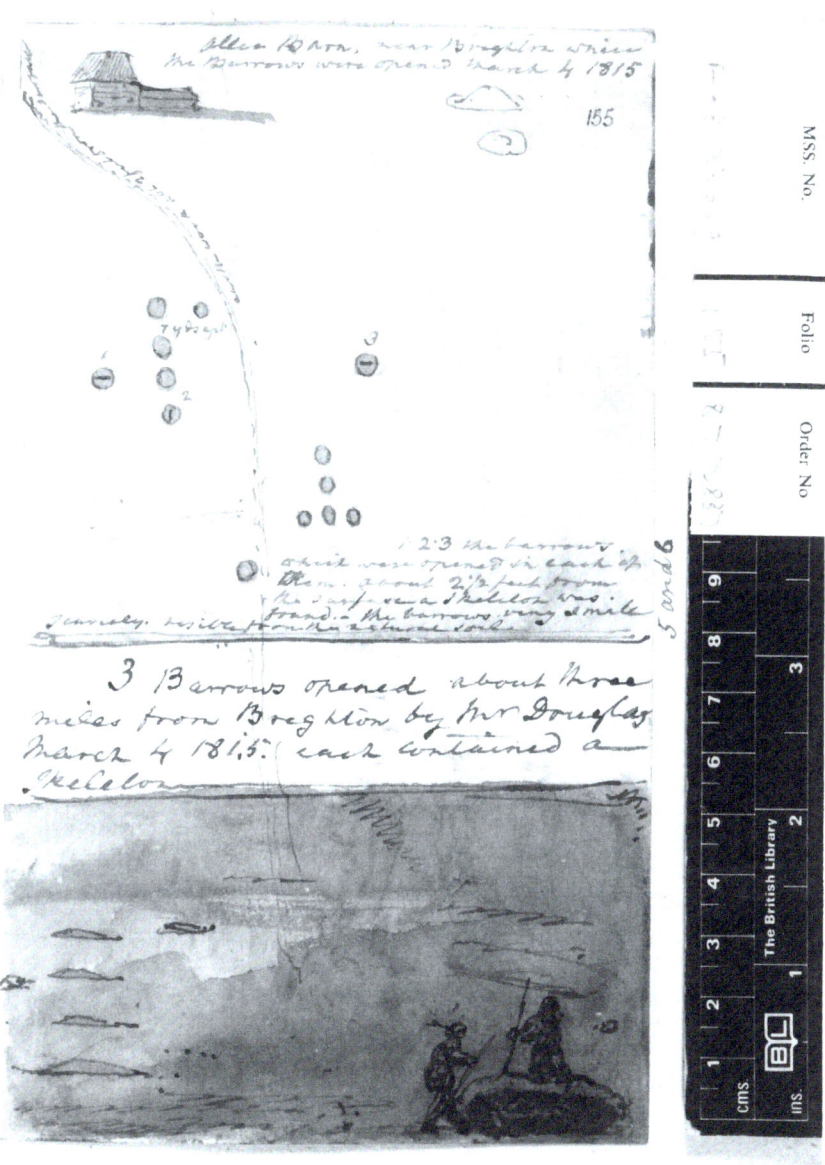

FIG.4. THE REVEREND SKINNER'S PLAN OF THE BARROW CEMETERY EXCAVATED ON THE 4TH MARCH 1815. (C.) THE BRITISH LIBRARY BOARD ADD 33658 F.155.

chalk. The head to the west; knife by the left side of iron – at the feet a small fragment of iron, with decayed wood adhering to it: teeth much decayed and the enamel much worn by mastication; evincing an old subject. The size of the bones indicating those of a male adult. (See the position of the skeletons on Baal's down, the head to the east.
The party consisted of Mrs D, Mrs R.D. my son Richard, Mr Stevens, Mr Fowle man servant, Mr Conoly – the shepherd and two of Ayre's boys'.

The second account is in a letter to the Rev. John Skinner dated the same day and supplies additional information:

'I am just returned from opening a Barrow situated on the Downs to the East above my Village only ¾ of a mile distant...... but my discoveries can by no means class with those of the Old British Chieftains being of a more modern date. It classes with the order of those on Baal's down near Brighton which you visited; but was near no groups of a bell fashioned beautiful form. The head of the skeleton was to the West in an opposite direction to those which you were at the opening of. On the left side, a knife about six inches in length of iron, with a buckle of the same; and at the feet a small piece of iron with decayed wood adhering to it – by which indicia I expected other relics'.

These burials were almost certainly Early or Middle Saxon in date but we know nothing else about them.

2.6. Five bell barrows excavated on Balls Down 5th October 1815

There are two surviving accounts of this excavation, of which the first is in James Douglas's common-place book:

'Opened five bell barrows of the groupe 15 in number on Bel's down (Baals down) near the single barn 1 mile beyond the race course at Brighton. The one to the north of the groupe at the extremity produced a pair of sheers and a small knife. Skeleton perfect of a woman. Sheers and knife close to the pelvis or os coxigis. This barrow was situated three paces distant to the west from one before opened which contained a knife and a silver ring.
2. barrow of a male adult

2. The Excavations

FIG.5. JAMES DOUGLAS'S DRAWING OF AN INHUMATION IN ONE OF THE BARROWS EXCAVATED ON THE 4TH MARCH 1815.

> 3. barrow at the extremity of the groupe to the south contained the skeleton of a male adult, with an oval perforation on the skull one inch in length. ¾ breadth. Certainly so perforated before interment; the cranium very thick and the edges of the extracted part of the bone clean and accurately opened.
> 4. a few paces from No.3 – a knife bones female adult.
> 5. Skeleton on the right side left arm over the body.
> The party. Sir John Colville, Mrs Prince Hoare, Mr Haydon historical painter, Revd Mr Townsend and his brother. 4 labourers of the veteran corps. Captain Bromley rode up'.

The second account is in the letter written by Douglas to Skinner on the 13th November 1815 (BM ADD MS 33665 p.10):

> 'On the 19th of June, on Fore Hill, to the east of this village, I opened a beautiful Bell Barrow of the lower order, in which as I conjectured, I found a skeleton, iron knife, and other relics of the same metal, which classes with the same Barrows on Belsdown, some of which we opened when you were present, and which group I completely opened October 5th, that is, the remaining four, two of which contained knives, and two iron buckles; one a pair of shears, similar to those discovered in tumuli of this order on Chatham Downs near Canterbury, engraved in Nen: Brit: one skeleton on the right side, left arm over the body – all the heads to the West: These Barrows date to the lowest aera of burial on waste lands – as low as the Heptarchy'.

Fig.6 also includes the barrows excavated on October 5th. These appear to be Middle Saxon in date.

2.7. Barrow on Church Hill, Brighton excavated 21st October 1815

There are three accounts of this excavation, with the first being in the common-place book:

> 'Opened the barrow to the south of the large barrow on the heighest top of the hill. The urn inverted; contained ashes of an adult perfectly blanched through a most ardent fire.

2. The Excavations

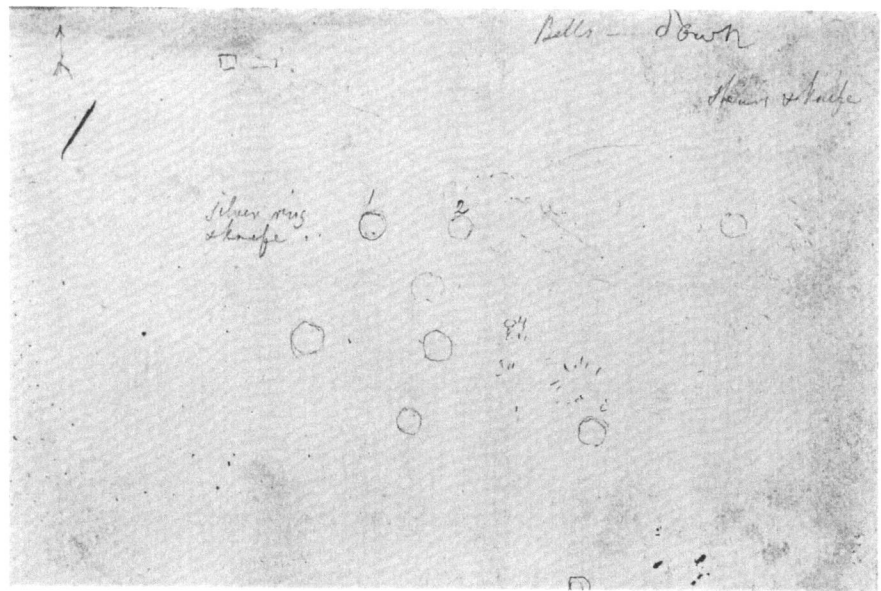

FIG.6. JAMES DOUGLAS'S PLAN OF PART OF THE BALSDEAN BARROW CEMETERY.

Primary interment. Urn; one foot 5 inches in height diameter 1 foot 3 inches the mouth (Fig.7). Circular cist in the chalk, sufficiently capacious to contain the mouth of the urn. Of the highest british order, of unbaked clay and similar to urns of this order found in various counties of this island. Subsequent interment in the above barrow. Bones of a skeleton Fistular bone apparently of a woman. Two brass buckles of the shape of Fig.1 and 2. Lower order of saxon burial.vid,Nen; Brit: The interment about one foot depth from the sod. This interment classes with the small skeleton barrows in groupes of the very lowest period of burial on waste lands; date 160 years from St Augustin advent and Ethelberts conversion to anno 800 of the Heptarchy see Nen: Brit: observations on small barrows in groupes' (Fig.8). Small bones from exuvia - rabbit or rat.

The second account is in the same letter to Skinner as the above:

'21st October 1815. Opened the large Barrow to the south of the largest Barrow on the Apex of the Church Hill: anout one foot under the turf of the centre of the Apex a skeleton much decomposed - two circular brass

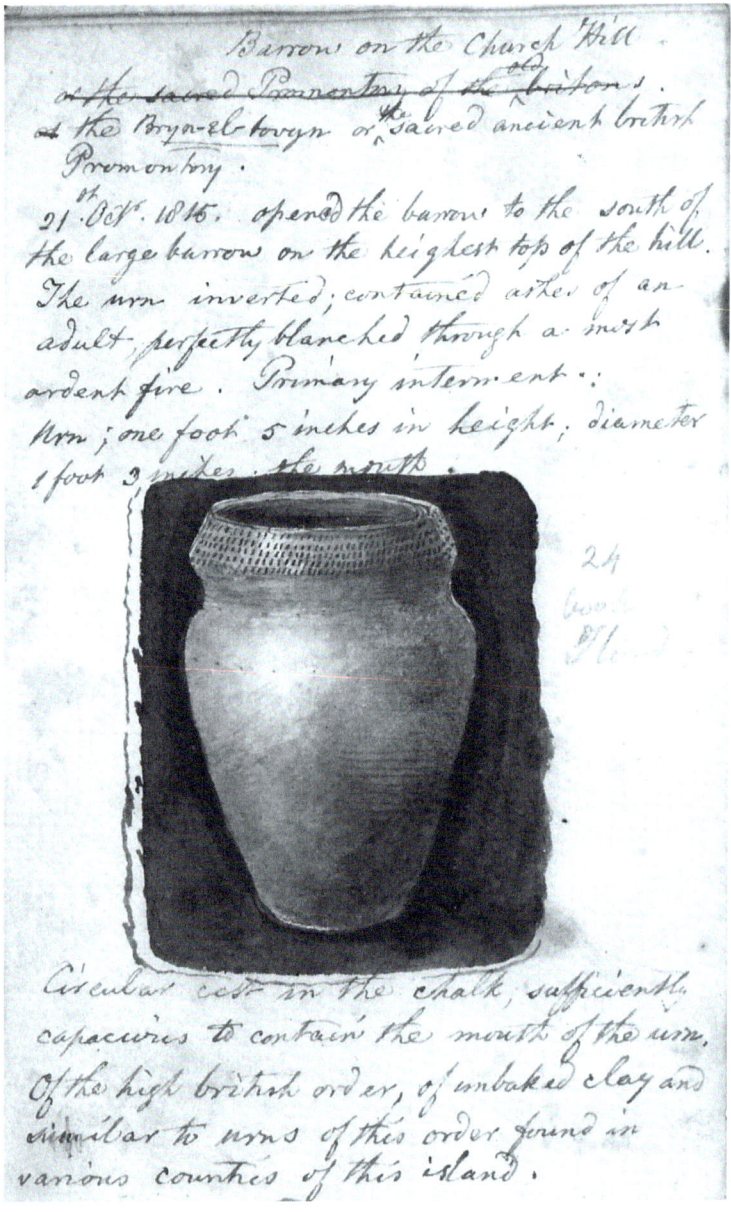

FIG.7. THE FIRST PART OF JAMES DOUGLAS'S ACCOUNT OF THE BARROW EXCAVATION ON CHURCH HILL, BRIGHTON WITH DRAWING OF COLLARED-URN.

buckles. This interment classes with the lowest order. Under this interment 3 feet the primary, British Urn, inverted over ashes, which had passed a most ardent fire – Cist excavated in the Chalk for the reception of the mouth of the urn.'

The third account is more entertaining than instructive and is in the autobiography of Benjamin Haydon the painter (1853, p.295).

'I went to Brighton, and invited Wilkie to come down, as I had met with a singular character in a friend of Prince Hoare's, the Rev.Mr Douglas, author of 'Naenia Britannica', an antiquary and an original.
Wilkie was delighted with Douglas, who put him in mind of the Vicar of Wakefield. Prince Hoare, Douglas and we two spent many pleasant days, and as Douglas greatly excited our curiosity about urn burials, we plagued him until he agreed to get leave to open the great barrow on the hill close to the church. We got leave, and also by permission of the colonel of the 10th, some of his men to dig for us, and early in the morning we set to work. Douglas, being commander, told us to let the men dig carefully till they found an urn upside down, and then dig round it most carefully till it was removed. We did so, and about noon came to an urn of unbaked clay, graceful in form and ornamented like a British shield: against Douglas's arrival it was ready for him; up he took it. 'There's iron said I; 'I hope not', thundered Douglas. He was so nervous to examine he broke the urn and out rolled the burnt bones of a human skeleton.
Douglas's theory was that at that early period brass was only in use; had it been iron I took up there would have been an end of his theory. By this time people crowded up the hill, and, it being cockney season, the cockneys who flocked round began to steal the bones. Wilkie was in ecstasies;- Hoare shrunk always at a crowd;- I took care of the urn, bought a muffin basket of a boy, and put it under Hoare's care. Douglas, now his antiquarian theory was safe, jumped into the grave and addressed the people on the wickedness of disturbing the ashes of the dead. Wilkie was delighted and kept saying 'Dear, dear,-look at him'. The effect of his large sack of a body, his small head, white hair and reverend look, his spectacles low down on his nose, and his grave expression as he eyed the mob over them, was indescribable. After a long harangue he persuaded the vulgar rich to stand back, and

> ordered the hussars to cover up the bones with respect. I believe in the long run there was only a finger or two missing, for many threw back their pilferings at the solemn injunctions of the antiquary'.

A second painting of the urn is bound into the back of the page proofs of Nenia Britannica, also in the author's possession.

The barrow was of the platform variety, approximately 39' in diameter, of indeterminate but considerable elevation, and one of the largest in a barrow cemetery north of St.Nicolas church. The urn containing the primary interment belongs to Longworth's primary collared series (1984) and can be dated c.2000-1750 BC. The two annular brooches associated with the secondary inhumation indicate that it was of a woman and are now in the Ashmolean Museum (MacGregor and Bolick 1993, 10.46 and 10.50). The photograph of the right-hand example of a pair of annular brooches from Sancton in Yorkshire (10.46) is identical to Douglas's right-hand illustration in the common-place book (Fig.8) and has clearly become muddled with one of the Sancton examples: another unprovenanced annular brooch alleged to be from the James Douglas collection (10.51) is identical to the other Sancton example and probably belongs there. There are two very similar brooches associated with Early Saxon Inhumation 24 in the Spong Hill cemetery, North Elmham, Norfolk (Hills et al 1984,Fig.80), indicating a c.AD.450-600 date-range for the type.

2.8. Two barrows at Black rock bottom excavated March 1816

There are two accounts of this excavation. The first of these is a very terse account in the common-place book with rather shaky drawings of the urns discovered (Fig.9):

> 'Opened two barrows. Urns of the higher order with ashes'.

The second account is in a letter by Douglas to the Rev.John Skinner dated 28th June 1816.

> 'Since I communicated to you the discovery of the fine British urn on the Church hill I opened two large British barrows in Black rock bottom to the left of the road from Brighthelmstone to Ratten dean – vulgarly called

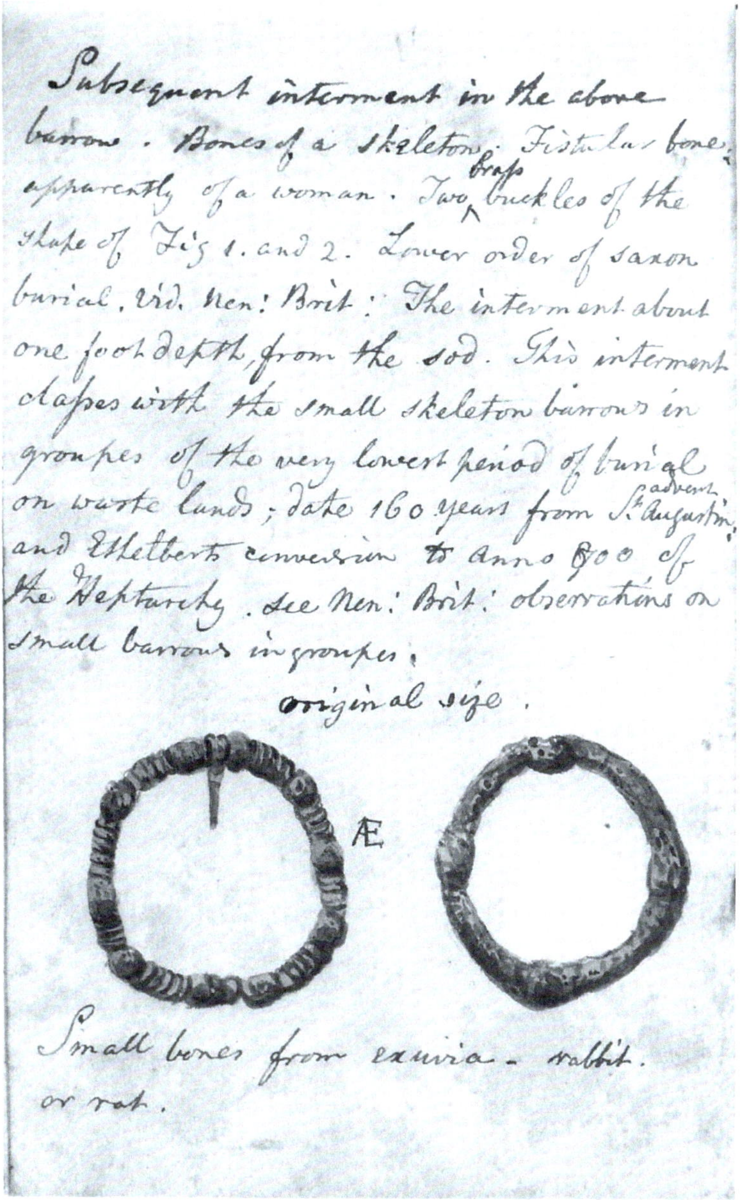

2. The Excavations 21

> Subsequent interment in the above barrow. Bones of a skeleton. Fistula bone, apparently of a woman. Two brass buckles of the shape of Fig 1. and 2. Lower order of Saxon burial. vid. Nen: Brit: The interment about one foot depth, from the sod. This interment clases with the small skeleton barrows in groupes of the very lowest period of burial on waste lands; date 160 years from S:t Augustin's advent and Ethelbert's conversion to anno 800 of the Heptarchy. See Nen: Brit: observations on small barrows in groupes.
>
> original size.
>
> Æ
>
> Small bones from exuvia - rabbit. or rat.

FIG.8. THE SECOND PART OF THE ACCOUNT WITH DRAWINGS OF TWO EARLY SAXON ANNULAR BROOCHES FROM SECONDARY INHUMATION.

FIG.9. TWO URNS FROM BLACK ROCK BOTTOM.

> *Rottendean. I found two large urns inverted over the ashes – of the highest order. A few days since I opened two others – no urns – but burnt bones and fragments of British Urns'.*

The two urns are shown inverted but appear to have been early collared examples with decoration on their shoulders (c.2000-1750 BC).

2.9. Barrows on Iford Down excavated in the spring of 1817

This excavation is recorded in a letter written by Douglas to Skinner on the 18th June 1817:

> *'About two months since I opened some interesting Barrows on Iford Down, a few miles from Brighton. Lower Romanised British – British and Skeleton Barrows of the lower order. Apropos, I wish you would direct your attention to these lower ones, in groups – sometimes solitary – and near the Old British, you will doubtless discover them. They teem with swords – bosses of shields – or the Umbones spears etc. Those of the Women, with beads, brooches, coins, and various most interesting relics: where the one was discovered of the bead you sent me a drawing of, is one of this order; and on the same spot I am convinced more will be found if search is undertaken. The tumulus by cultivation is frequently levelled; but an iron crow will easily define the cist, from the native soil or stratum'.*

All of Douglas's letters to Skinner exist as copies made by the latter in his journals. There follows a key to a map sent by Douglas, which unfortunately was not reproduced by Skinner.

The Iford Down Barrows

A. *Romano British – small Urn and burnt bones. Small buckles of brass and iron. Melted vessels of brass.*
B. *Square Barrow – the trench square: found in other places on the Sussex Downs.*
C. *Skeleton Barrow with a gold pendant on the breast: head to the west.*
D. *Skeleton Barrow: head to the north – near to which a small arferial or lustral vessel.*
E. *E E. British Barrows of the higher order*

F. British Track Way.
G. British or Belgic entrenchment.
H. An Agger of flint which in Wiltshire is called a Linch and in these parts Lincs.

The gold pendant is in the Ashmolean Museum (Macgregor and Bolick 1993, 25.2) and illustrated in the commonplace book (Fig.10). It is described as being of sheet metal with four concentric rings of beaded wire applied to its obverse. There are four S-scrolls of beaded wire within the inner pair of rings and eight more within the outer pair. The object could be described as a bracteate and is of 5th-to-7th c. date.

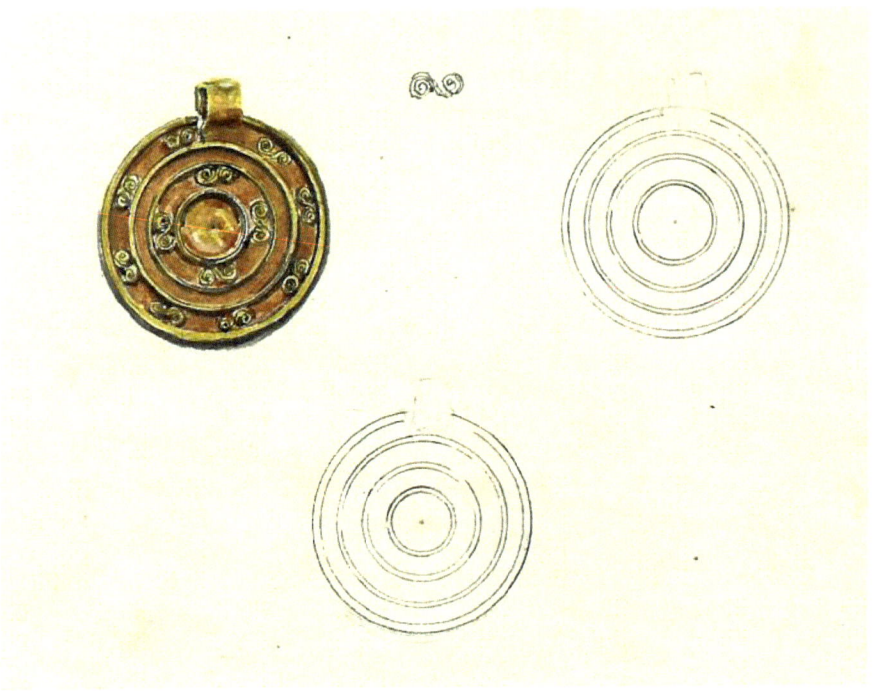

FIG.10. GOLD 'BRACTEATE' FROM IFORD HILL BARROW.

2.10. Miscellaneous

The common-place book also contains two paintings and a sketch of unspecified barrow excavations in the Brighton area. One of the paintings appears to be of Douglas excavating a small barrow to the north-west of Brighton (Fig.11), with the town just visible in the distance on the left hand edge of the painting and the post mill figured in Fig.17 visible in the same direction. The other painting is unfinished and has been subsequently scribbled over by a ?child.

The sketch is very faint and shares a page with a much later doodle of a section through a tobacco pipe: this latter has been excised from the published drawing (Fig.12). There is nothing to indicate the location of the barrow but the drawing features two men, two women and a child at the excavation.

Fig.11. Water colour from the common-place book showing excavation of a small Saxon barrow north-west of Brighton.

FIG.12. SKETCH FROM THE COMMON-PLACE BOOK OF TWO MEN, TWO WOMEN AND A CHILD ATTENDING BARROW EXCAVATION AT AN UNSPECIFIED LOCATION NEAR BRIGHTON.

3. Megaliths in the Brighton area

3.1. The Goldstone at Hove

This large puddingstone megalith can be found illustrated in vignettes on maps of Sussex as far back as the 17th century and is accurately drawn in Douglas's common-place book (Fig.13): a less accurate water colour is also present in the same book (Fig.14). The drawing is important in that it dates to before the stone was overthrown and buried by a local farmer c.1834 and shows the stone to have stood on a small mound with other, smaller stones in its vicinity. The stone also had its long axis in the vertical plane; a position it is unlikely to have achieved by natural means and one which was not shared by most of the other puddingstone boulders which originally littered the area in a similar manner to the sarsens on Salisbury Plain.

The Goldstone was disinterred in 1902 and re-erected in Hove Park. A letter written by Douglas to Sir Richard Colt Hoare on the 25th June 1812 refers to his having dug around the Goldstone and not finding anything (Jessup 1975,272).

FIG.13. DRAWING OF THE GOLD STONE AT HOVE FROM THE COMMON-PLACE BOOK.

Fig.14. Water colour of the Gold Stone from the common-place book.

3.2. The ?stone circle in Goldstone Bottom to the north of the Goldstone

The common-place book contains a long section on the etymology of Sussex place-names which is reproduced below (pp.40-55, Figs.22-29). Most of Douglas's interpretations are fanciful nonsense but the entry for Brighthelm-stone includes the following:

> 'In the extremity of the valley to the north-east of this stone (The Goldstone), where the two men of the Oxford Militia were shot for mutiny, there are the dilapidated remains of a cirque'.

This cirque was the subject of a drawing by the local artist H.G.Hine made in 1828 and entitled 'Ancient Stones. Gouldstone Bottom' (Toms 1927). The view looks west with the sea in the background and shows a man standing beside an upright stone of similar height to himself at the southern end of an arc of at least five or six smaller uprights spaced closely together. A number of other large recumbent stones were scattered around this feature, which lay in close proximity to a pond.

It is difficult to believe that the upright stones could have arrived at their positions by natural means but we will never know for certain as they were removed in 1847 and the pond filled in.

3.3. The barrow cemetery and stones north of St. Nicholas church, Brighton

Both James Douglas and Skinner make reference to the stones.

The common-place book has the following entry under Brighthelmstone in the etymological section of the notebook:

> 'On the hill west of Brighton church close to the London Roman road are several large stones on some celtic barrows. Their composition is of large Silex bolters imbedded in arenaceous iron grit; excavated from the secondary deposit in the chalk valleys. They have been undermined and were originally placed on the apix of the british sepulchre. There is also one of these stones with some fragments to the east side of the London road on the slope of the hill opposite the farmhouse of Mr Murrel, a tenant of Mr Kemp the Sussex member. There is also a considerable larger one with several fragments on the land of Mr Stamford in the parish of Hove, which goes by the name of Goldstone'.

The Rev. John Skinner had visited the site in 1815 on his first visit to Brighton but returned again in February 1821, nearly two years after Douglas's death. He gave the following account in his journal:

> 'February 14th
> There is another circumstance which induces me to think that Brighton was a place of considerable importance in the time of the Belgic Britons; which is, the remains of Druidical stones on the hill where the Church now stands. This place I visited in the company of Mr Douglas, six years since, and I again examined the spot, on quitting Wick hill today. The summit of Church hill, for so it is now called, was secured to the west by a high agger, where the ground was less steep; the bank was double within this fence, near where a windmill has been recently erected: there are three Tumuli; one 80 paces in circuit, one 60, and the third 40. One of the barrows, which has been dug into, exhibits a rough stone, weighing nearly half a ton, with two smaller near it, which seem to have been used to form a Cistvaen

to receive the urn and ashes of the deceased. Near to this barrow, on a small mound (but not a place of interment) there is a large stone of an irregular form, about seven feet and a half in length, and six in the widest part, in breadth: it appears to have been originally one of the supporters of a Cromlech. There is a tradition, that several stones of a similar kind (that is of silicious boulters imbedded in very hard iron grit) were formerly on this height but gradually used by persons in the neighbourhood for building. If the Druids had a Cromlech on this spot, it was in all probability accompanied by a circle'.

Skinner produced two drawings of the barrow cemetery during his first visit in 1815. These include a panoramic view looking north-west from the tower of St Nicholas Church (Fig.15) and showing four round barrows and a square one (BM ADD MS 33649, Folio 151). One of the round barrows in the

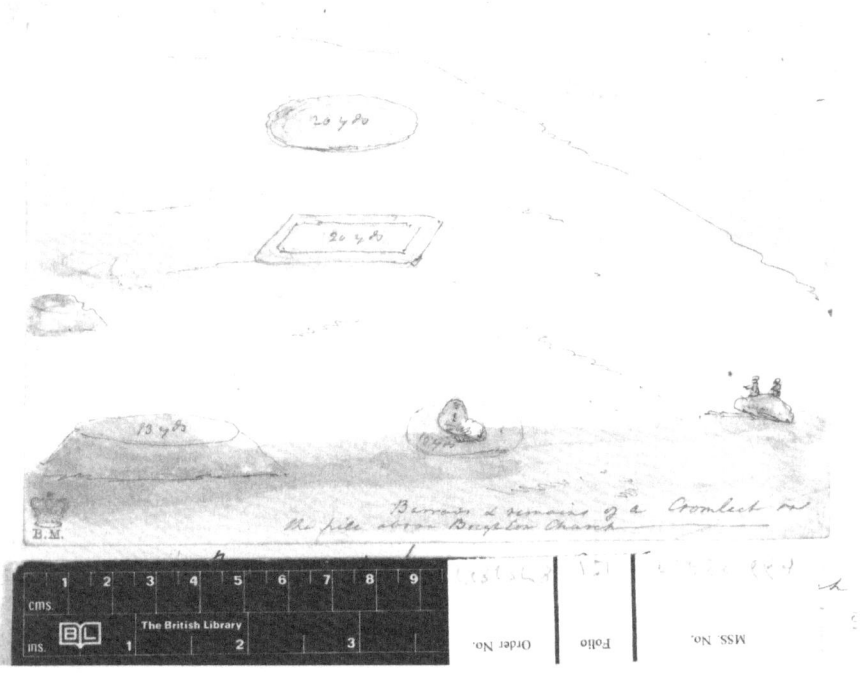

FIG.15. PANORAMIC VIEW OF BARROW CEMETERY AND 'CROMLECH' ON CHURCH HILL MADE BY SKINNER LOOKING NORTH FROM CHURCH TOWER. (C.) THE BRITISH LIBRARY BOARD ADD 33649 F.151.

3. Megaliths in the Brighton area 31

foreground is shown as 10 yards in diameter with the large stone, thought by Skinner to be part of a Cistvaen, in its centre. The platform barrow to its west and indicated as being 13 yards in diameter is almost certainly that dug by Douglas on the 21st October 1815 after Skinner's visit. The large stone which Skinner thought was part of a cromlech is also shown with two people seated on it.

Square barrows are concentrated in East Yorkshire and thought to be of Iron Age date. There are a few in the south-east of Britain as well, including the example on Church hill and another on Iford Down referred to above.

The second drawing (Fig.16) is a view south-east towards the church with the barrow dug by Douglas and a smaller one to its north-west in the foreground (BM.ADD MS 33649, Folio 145).

Skinner produced a further two drawings on his second visit in 1821; both of which are dated February 14th. The first of these (BM ADD MS

FIG.16. VIEW OF SAME BARROWS LOOKING SOUTH-EAST TOWARDS CHURCH. (C.) THE BRITISH LIBRARY BOARD ADD 33649 F.145.

33658, Folio 27) is entitled *'Tumuli on Church hill near the windmill'* and is a panoramic view to the south-west depicting the 'cromlech', 'cistvaen' and barrow excavated by Douglas, with the windmill to their west and another round barrow in the distance. The measurements given against the various barrows appear to be circumferences rather than the diameters given on the earlier drawing (Fig.17). The second drawing (Ibid., Folio 30) is a close-up of the 'cistvaen' and is entitled *'Barrow on Church hill with three stones*

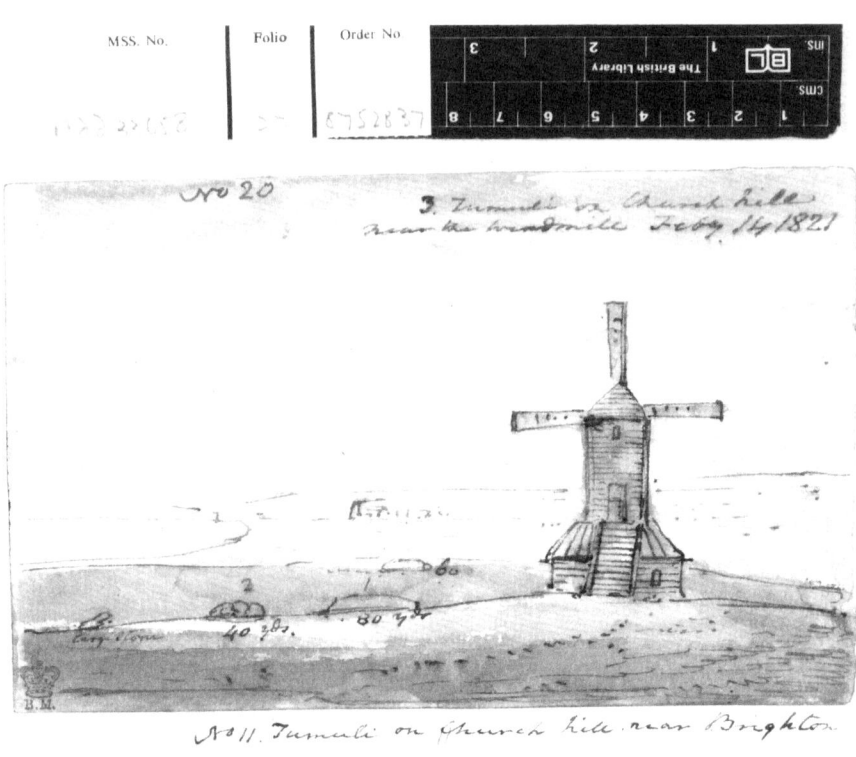

Fig.17. View of same barrows and 'cromlech' looking west along coast towards Wick Hall, Hove with post mill in foreground. (c.) The British Library Board Add 33658 f.27.

3. Megaliths in the Brighton area

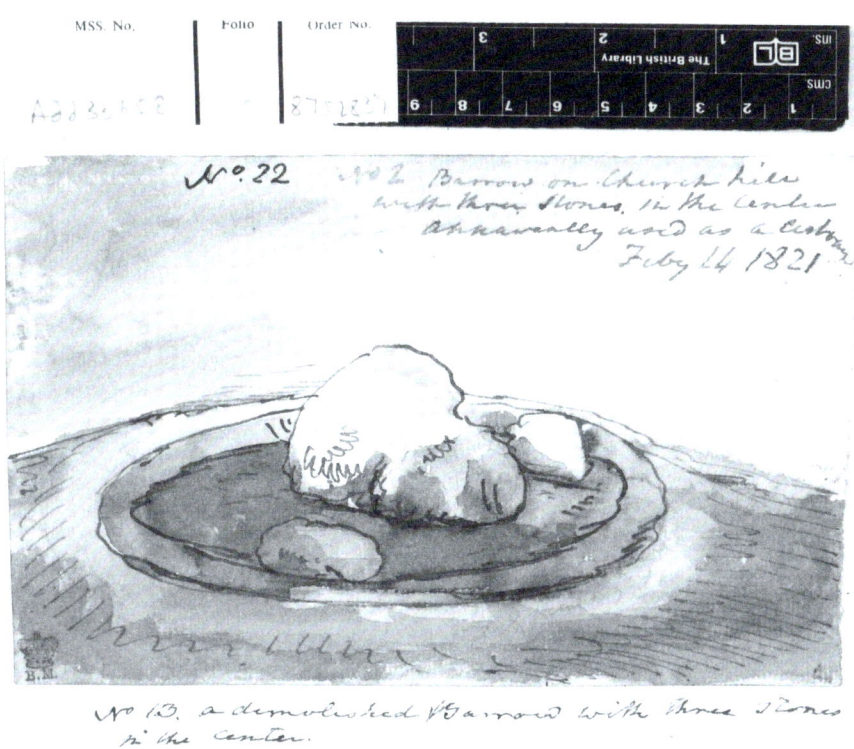

Fig.18. Close up view by Skinner of 'cromlech' on Church Hill. (c.) The British Library Board Add 33658 f.30

in the center apparently used as a cistvaen'. The circular ditch around these stones is clearly delineated, although there is no obvious indication of the barrow itself (Fig.18). The largest of these stones is also drawn from two different angles by Douglas in his common-place book with the heading *'Church hill South E of the great barrow nearby'* (Figs.19 and 20). An untitled sepia-wash drawing of a similarly-shaped stone with four people around it (Fig.21) may also be of the same, although bushes in the background do not appear in any other of the illustrations.

FIG.19. DRAWING FROM COMMON-PLACE BOOK BY JAMES DOUGLAS OF LARGE 'CROMLECH' STONE VIEWED FROM SOUTH.

FIG.20. VIEW OF SAME STONE FROM NORTH.

3. Megaliths in the Brighton area

FIG.21. DRAWING FROM COMMON-PLACE BOOK OF TWO MEN AND TWO BOYS AROUND LARGE STONE, WHICH FROM ITS SHAPE COULD BE THE LARGEST ONE IN THE 'CROMLECH' ON CHURCH HILL.

4. Sussex Placename derivations and miscellania

Seventeen pages in the commonplace book are given over to Sussex place-name derivations (Figs. 22-30). The entries indicate that Douglas had access to a number of relevent publications, including William Borlase 1754 *Observations on the antiquities historical and monumental of the county of Cornwall*, Edward Lluyd 1707 *Archaeologia Britannica: an Account of the Languages, Histories and Customs of Great Britain*, Walter Whiter 1800 *Etymologicon Magnum* and John Speed 1611 *Historie of Great Britaine*. He believed, along with many of his contemporaries, that the world's languages were all descended from one proto-language but, unlike modern researchers into Proto-Indo-European, had no concept as to the period of time involved.

Douglas lived in a world where most people believed that the act of creation took place over six days in 4004 BC and that the diffusion of languages took place somewhat more recently. Most etymologists today believe that the specific development of Indo-European languages took place between 10000 and 3500 BC and could have started even earlier. Douglas's mistake was to seek elements from a variety of these already-developed languages such as Armorican, British, Cornish, Irish, Greek and Hebrew in many Sussex place-names because he regarded these languages as still developing out of his proto-language at the time of the place-names coming into being. This renders James Douglas's interpretations of little use today, although it does shine a light on the etymological reasoning prevalent at his time and shared with Edward Lluyd and others.

Some of Douglas's place-name interpretations managed to make it into print in an article by him in the first edition of the Provincial Magazine (1818) and eventually outlived him in successive editions of a popular history of Brighton (Sicklemore 1827, 1-5).

This etymological section in the common-place book is interrupted by a note on the current state of palaeontological and geological studies, including a section on Cuvier's discovery of the *Palaeotherium* in the Eocene gypsum deposits of the Paris Basin. The note relates to another of James Douglas's range of interests; that of earth sciences. He had already published a paper on the subject (Douglas 1785) in which he came to the conclusion that the earth was far older than previously thought. The entry in the common-place book is worth publishing in full:

Fossil bones of Hippopotamus.
Lt. Fauja de Saint Fond says in Essais de Geologie T.1. p.364 et suis qu'il n'a rien vu dans les cabinets qu'il a visites dans ses voyages, en dans les auteurs qu'il a consultes d'on l'on puifre conelure que l'hippopotame se soit trouve jusqu'a present dans l'etat fossile avec les elephans, les rhinoceros et les autres grands quadrupeds des pays chaudes.
Animal de Simome An. Incog. differing from the Ohio animal Incognitum vulgarly called Mammouth the name given by the Indiens. Cuvier has given the name of grand Palaeotherium, an an'. Incogn: see the institute 1805 Tome Sixieme. Also page 104 of another vol. The Simome of Cuvier differ from the Hippopotamus. p.105.
Aldrovandenus has compared the tooth of the Hip: with that of the Elephant – see also Ph. Trans:
Aldrovan; de metallices lib.IV. p.228. et suiv. See also Tab VI. Fig. 1. see Daubenton. Cabinet of M. Gowan Montpellier. Small Hippopot. the size of a wild boar – see Cuvier – p 117. Institut.
A paper of Peron – to Le Mark on the declension of the ocean by the increase of Madropores, Corals or polypi. of the Pacif. Ocean to prove these animals found fossil in Europe attest the equatorial changes of the globe.
The sarique of Vergine found in the Gypsum hill near Paris, see Inst: p.281. The remit of this discovery is viz: qu'il y a dans les carrieres a platre qui environment Paris, a un grand profondeur et sous diverses couches remplies des coquillages marins, des animaux qui ne peuvent etre que d'un genere aujourdhui entierement particulier a l'Amerique, ou d'un autre entierement particulier a la Nouvelle Hollande. 5 vol. of the Institut. of Paris.

This entry is full of abbreviations and difficult to read but gives a fascinating view of the level of knowledge of both geology and palaeontology at the beginning of the 19th century. The various people referred to in the entry read like a who's who of pioneer naturalists, palaeontologists and geologists.

Barthelemy Faujas de Saint-Fond (1741-1819) was a pioneer geologist and traveller who saw the contents of many cabinets of curiosities during his trips around Europe. These contents included fossil remains of elephants, rhinoceri and other large quadrupeds and raised the question as to what such beasts from tropical climes were doing in Europe.

Georges Cuvier (1769-1832) has been called the father of palaeontology and was responsible for naming as the *Palaeotherium* the fossil of a small early Eocene relative of the horse found in the gypsum beds of the Paris Basin, also referred to as a sarique or opossum elsewhere in the note. This was the first fossil mammal genus to be named, hence the rather simplistic choice of 'ancient beast'. When Cuvier examined mammoth remains found in Ohio, he simply classified them as being from the Grand *Palaeotherium* despite their very different nature. Cuvier was a catastrophist and believed that there had been a whole series of creations terminated by successive floods.

Ulysses Aldrovandi (1522-1605) was an Italian naturalist and one of the first whose writings are based on direct observation. This has led to him being called the father of natural history: he is also credited with coining the word 'geology'.

Lamarck (1744-1829, the Le Mark of James Douglas) could perhaps be regarded as the father of evolutionary theory, although his interpretations of the mechanisms behind evolution were faulty and both ridiculed and violently opposed by Cuvier. His pioneer work was, nevertheless, acknowledged by Charles Darwin sixty years later.

Francois Peron (1775-1810) was the zoologist on Nicolas Baudin's expedition to Australia and thought that the presence of fossil corals in Europe, similar to those found in the Pacific Ocean, attested to changes in the position of the equator. He had little opportunity to develop his theories, dying young from tuberculosis.

It is clear from this note in the common-place book that Douglas was well-read in the latest developments in the natural sciences: he had himself made a significant contribution in his 1785 publication 'A Dissertation on the Antiquity of the Earth' written before Cuvier and Lamarck had even commenced their researches.

The common-place book also contains a short note on ancient mirrors copied from a French publication, a recipe for china painting, a painting of a Maori tiki and a note on the creation of the white horse on Osmington Hill near Weymouth in 1808 when George III was there recovering from one of his bouts of insanity.

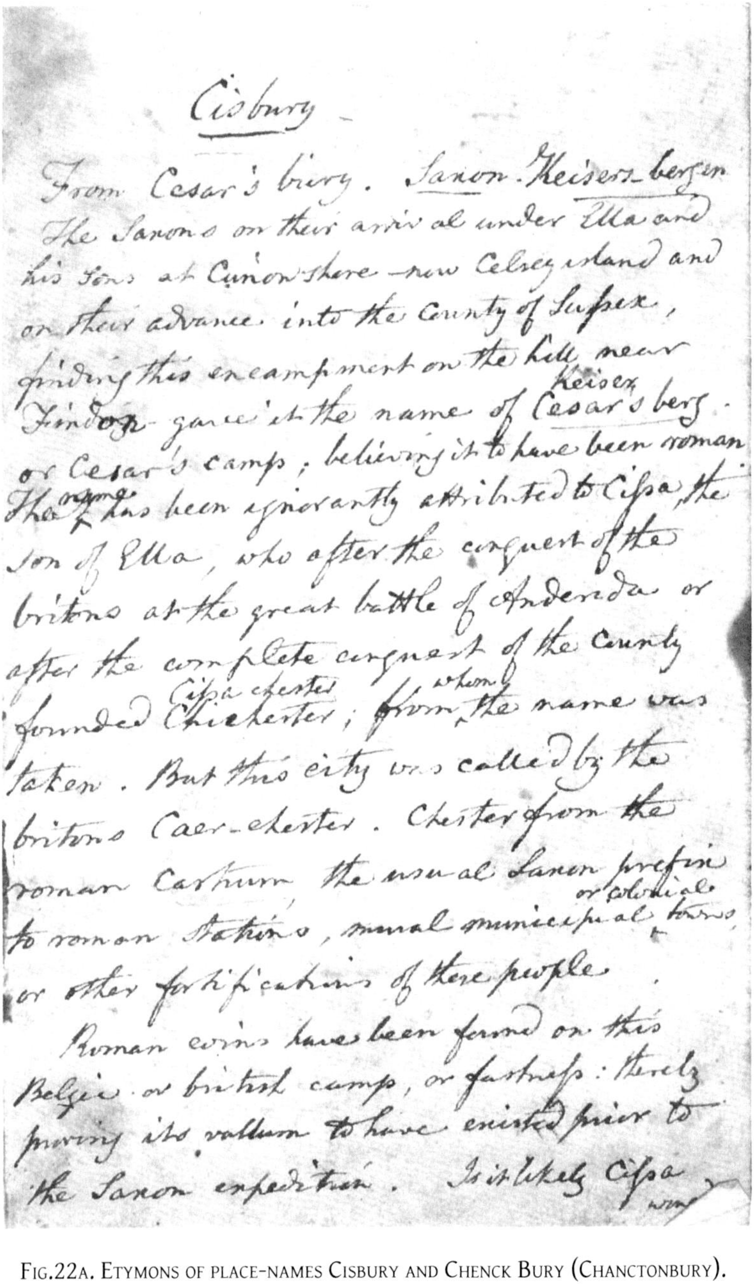

> Cisbury —
>
> From Cesar's bury. Saxon - Heisers-bergen
> The Saxons on their arrival under Ella and
> his sons at Cimon shore — now Celsey island and
> on their advance into the County of Sussex,
> finding this encampment on the hill near
> Findon gave it the name of Cesar's berg
> or Cesar's camp; believing it to have been roman.
> The name has been ignorantly attributed to Cissa, the
> son of Ella, who after the conquest of the
> britons at the great battle of Andenda or
> after the complete conquest of the County
> founded Chichester; from whom the name was
> taken. But this city was called by the
> britons Caer-chester. Chester from the
> roman Castrum, the usual Saxon prefix
> to roman stations, rural municipal towns,
> or other fortifications of these people.
>
> Roman coins have been found on this
> Belgic or british camp, or fastness: thereby
> proving its vallum to have existed prior to
> the Saxon expedition. Is it likely Cissa

FIG.22A. ETYMONS OF PLACE-NAMES CISBURY AND CHENCK BURY (CHANCTONBURY).

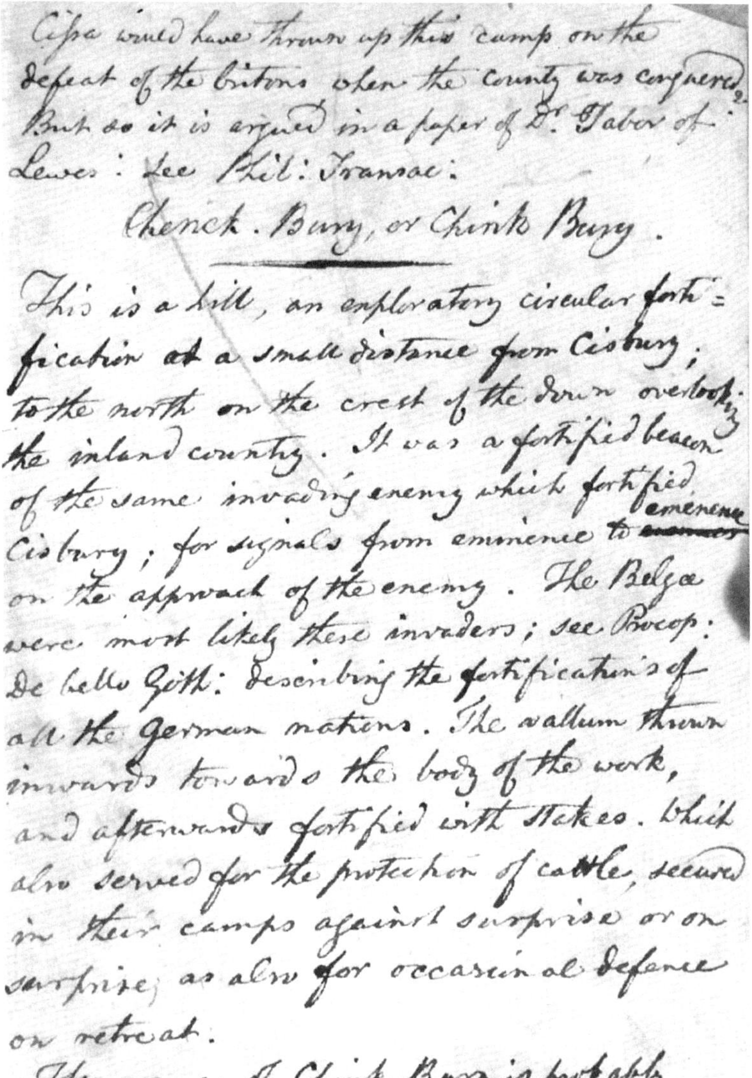

Cissa would have thrown up this camp on the defeat of the Britons when the county was conquered. But so it is argued in a paper of D.r Tabor of Lewes: see Phil: Transac:

Chenck. Bury, or Chink Bury.

This is a hill, an exploratory circular fortification at a small distance from Cisbury; to the north on the crest of the down overlooking the inland country. It was a fortified beacon of the same invading enemy which fortified Cisbury; for signals from eminence to eminence on the approach of the enemy. The Belgæ were most likely these invaders; see Procop: De bello Goth: describing the fortifications of all the German nations. The vallum thrown inwards towards the body of the work, and afterwards fortified with stakes. Which also served for the protection of cattle, secured in their camps against surprise or on surprise; as also for occasional defence on retreat.

The name of Chink Bury is probably derived from the armoric Cen and Cornish Cinkla to cast up. Bury or Burg the Saxon prefix

Fig.22b. Etymons of place-names Cisbury and Chenck Bury (Chanctonbury).

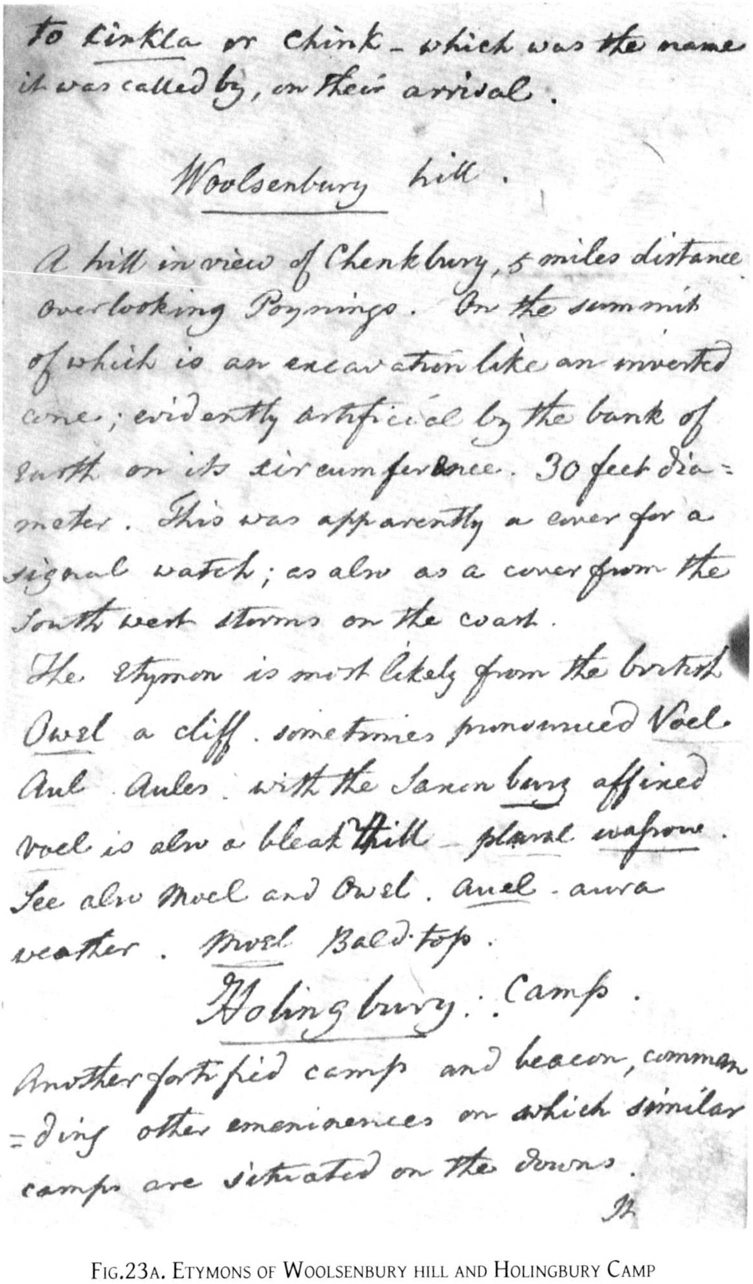

> to kinkla or chink — which was the name it was called by, on their arrival.
>
> Woolsenbury hill.
>
> A hill in view of Chenkbury, 5 miles distance overlooking Poynings. On the summit of which is an excavation like an inverted cone; evidently artificial by the bank of earth on its circumference. 30 feet diameter. This was apparently a cover for a signal watch; as also as a cover from the South west storms on the coast.
> The etymon is most likely from the british Owel a cliff. sometimes pronounced Voel. Aul Aules; with the Saxon bury affixed voel is also a bleak hill — plural wafowe. See also Moel and Owel. Auel — awra weather. Moel Bald-top.
>
> Holingbury. Camp.
> Another fortified camp and beacon, commanding other eminences on which similar camps are situated on the downs.

FIG.23A. ETYMONS OF WOOLSENBURY HILL AND HOLINGBURY CAMP

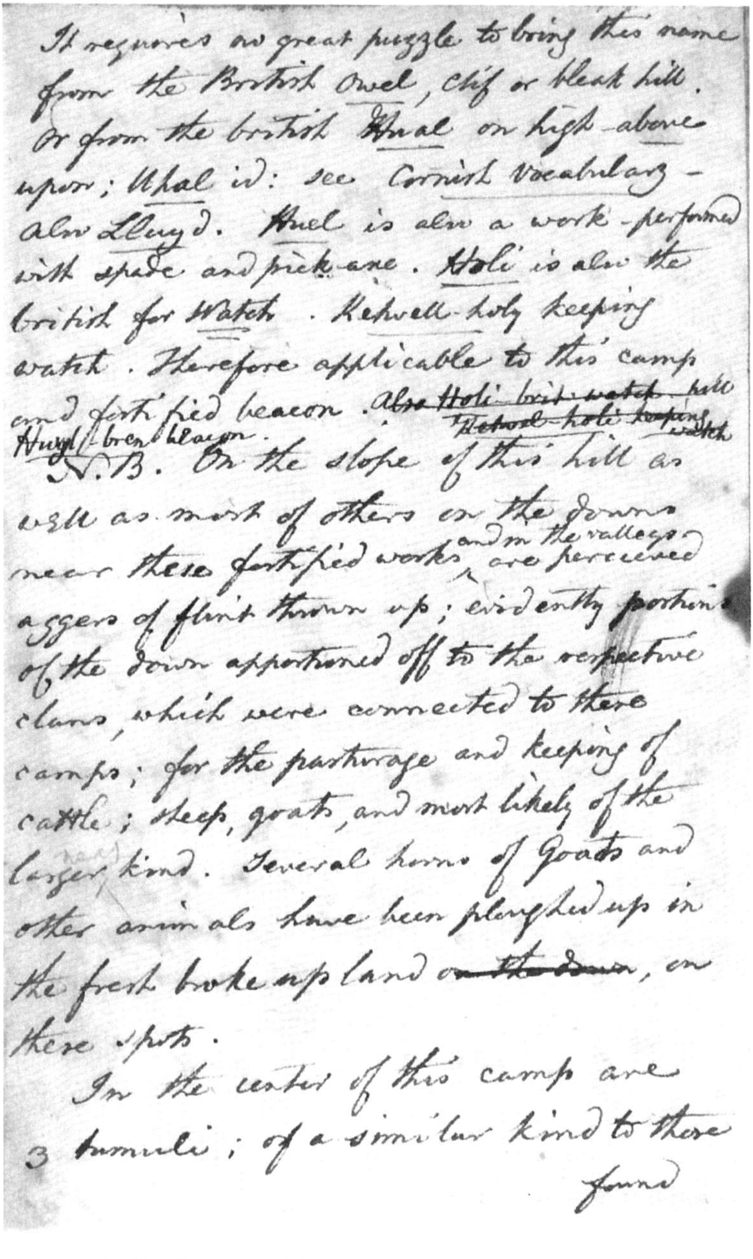

It requires no great puzzle to bring this name from the British Owel, clif or bleak hill. Or from the british Hual on high - above upon; Uhal id: see Cornish Vocabulary - also Lluyd. Huel is also a work - performed with spade and pick-axe. Holi is also the british for Watch. Hehwell-holy keeping watch. Therefore applicable to this camp and fortified beacon. Also Holi brit watch Hwyl-bren beacon. Hetwrd-hole keeping

N.B. On the slope of this hill as well as most of others on the downs near these fortified works, and in the valleys, are perceived aggers of flint thrown up; evidently portions of the down apportioned off to the respective clans, which were connected to these camps; for the pasturage and keeping of cattle; sheep, goats, and most likely of the larger kind. Several horns of goats and other animals have been ploughed up in the fresh broke up land on the down, on these spots.

In the center of this camp are 3 tumuli; of a similar kind to those found

FIG.23B. ETYMONS OF WOOLSENBURY HILL AND HOLINGBURY CAMP

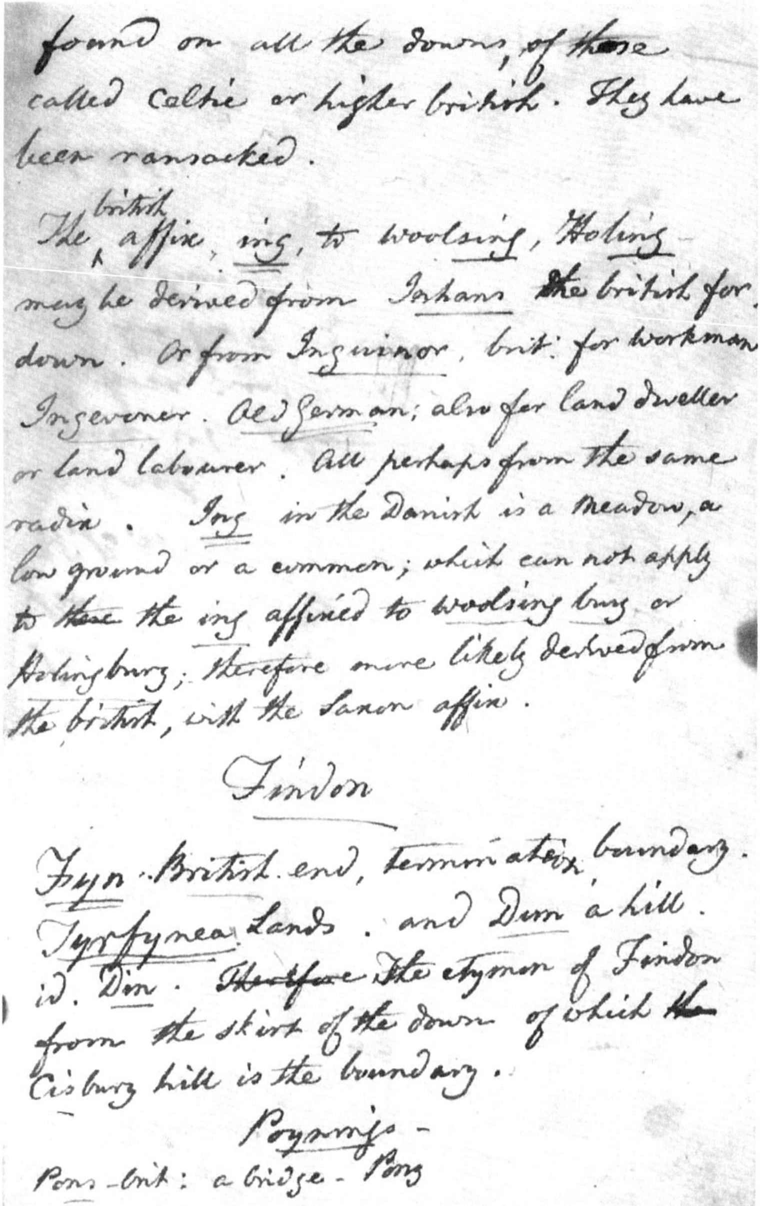

found on all the downs, of those called Celtic or higher british. They have been ransacked.

The british affix, ing, to woolsing, Holing may be derived from Inhans the british for down. Or from Inguinor, brit: for workman Ingevener. Old German; also for land dweller or land labourer. All perhaps from the same radix. Ing in the Danish is a meadow, a low ground or a common; which can not apply to these the ing affixed to woolsing bury, or Holingbury; therefore more likely derived from the british, with the Saxon affix.

Findon

Fyn – British. end, termination, boundary. Tyrfynea Lands. and Dun a hill. id. Din. Therefore the etymon of Findon from the skirt of the down of which the Cisbury hill is the boundary.

Poynings –
Pons – brit: a bridge – Pons

FIG. 24A. ETYMONS OF HOLINGBURY CAMP (CONTINUED), FINDON, POYNINGS, PULBOROUGH, BILLINGSHURST AND CLAYDON.

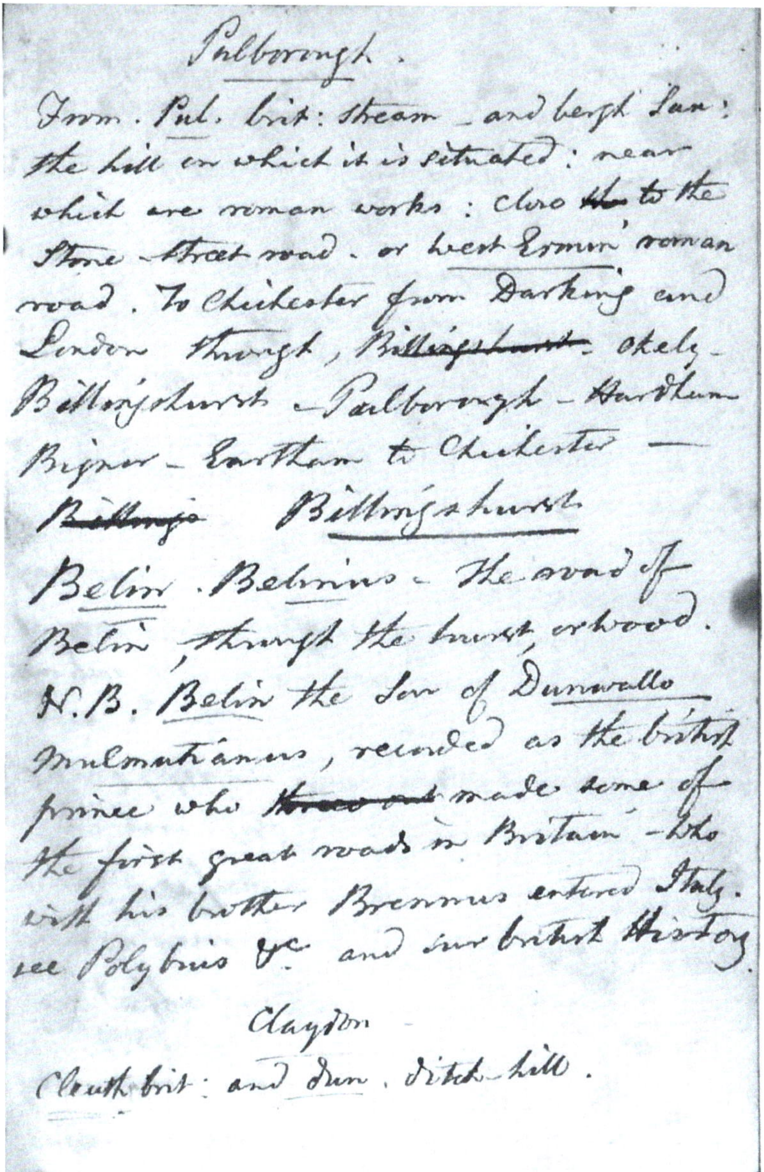

4. Sussex Placename derivations and miscellania

> Pulborough.
> From. Pul. brit: stream – and bergh Sax:
> the hill on which it is situated: near
> which are roman works: close to the
> Stone-street road – or West Ermin roman
> road. To Chichester from Dorking and
> London through, ~~Billingshurst~~ Okely-
> Billingshurst – Pulborough – Hardham
> Bignor – Eartham to Chichester –
>
> ~~Billings~~   Billingshurst
> Belin. Belinus – the road of
> Belin, through the hurst, or wood.
> N.B. Belin the Son of Dunwallo
> Mulmatianus, recorded as the british
> prince who ~~through~~ made some of
> the first great roads in Britain – who
> with his brother Brennus entered Italy.
> see Polybius &c. and our british History.
>
> Claydon –
> Cleuth brit: and Dun. ditch-hill.

FIG.24B. ETYMONS OF HOLINGBURY CAMP (CONTINUED), FINDON, POYNINGS, PULBOROUGH, BILLINGSHURST AND CLAYDON.

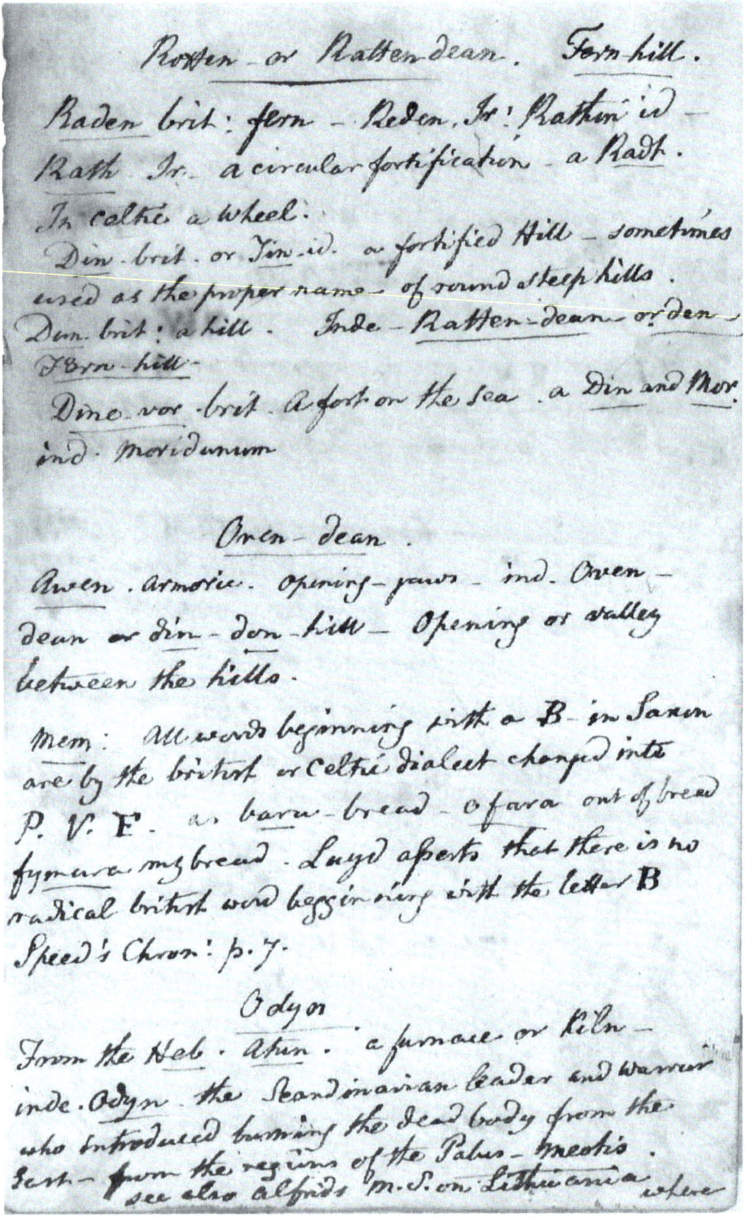
Rotten - or Ratten dean. Fern hill.

Raden brit: fern - Reden. Ir: Rathen id -
Rath. Ir. a circular fortification - a Radt.
In celtic a wheel.
Din - brit. or Tin - id. a fortified Hill - sometimes
used as the proper name of round steep hills.
Dun. brit: a hill. Inde - Ratten - dean - or den -
Fern - hill -
Dine - vor - brit. A fort on the sea. a Din and Mor.
ind. Moridunum

Oven - dean.

Awen. armoric. Opening - jaws - ind. Oven -
dean or din - don - hill - Opening or valley
between the hills.

Mem: All words beginning with a B - in Saxon
are by the british or Celtic dialect changed into
P. V. F. as bara - bread - o fara out of bread
fymara my bread. Luyd asserts that there is no
radical british word beginning with the letter B
Speed's Chron: p. 7.

Odyor

From the Heb. Atun. a furnace or kiln -
inde. Odyn the Scandinavian leader and warrior
who introduced burning the dead body from the
East - from the regions of the Palus - Meotis.
see also Alfrid's M.S. on Lithuania where

Fig.25a. Etymons of Rotten or Rattendean, Oven dean, Odyor and Patcham where the custom of burning the dead, was continued to this day An: 889. This appears to have been a clan of the same colony which Odin transported from the Chersonesis. The Geographic situation will prove this; and which may account for the two ages of the Danish and Norwegian history. The age of burning - &fire, and the age of burial. The brend tide - and Hoel tide Brigold and Hoelgold. The age of hills also and the age of shovels.

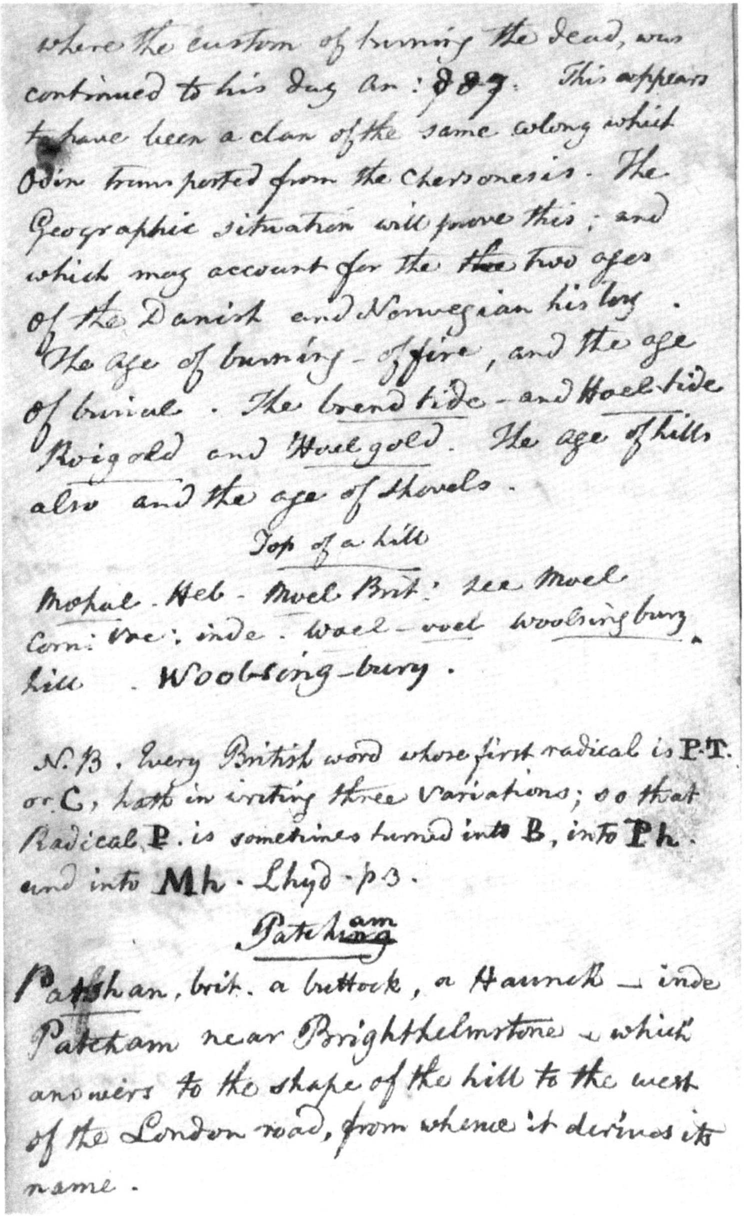

   Top of a hill

Mohal. Heb - Moel Brit: see Moel Corn: ire: inde. Wael—voel Woolsingbury. hill. Woolsing-bury.

N.B. Every British word whose first radical is P.T. or C, hath in writing three Variations; so that Radical P. is sometimes turned into B, into Ph. and into Mh. Lhyd - p.3.

   Patcham

Patshan, brit. a buttock, a Haunch — inde Patcham near Brighthelmstone — which answers to the shape of the hill to the west of the London road, from whence it derives its name.

FIG.25B. ETYMONS OF ROTTEN OR RATTENDEAN, OVEN DEAN, ODYOR AND PATCHAM

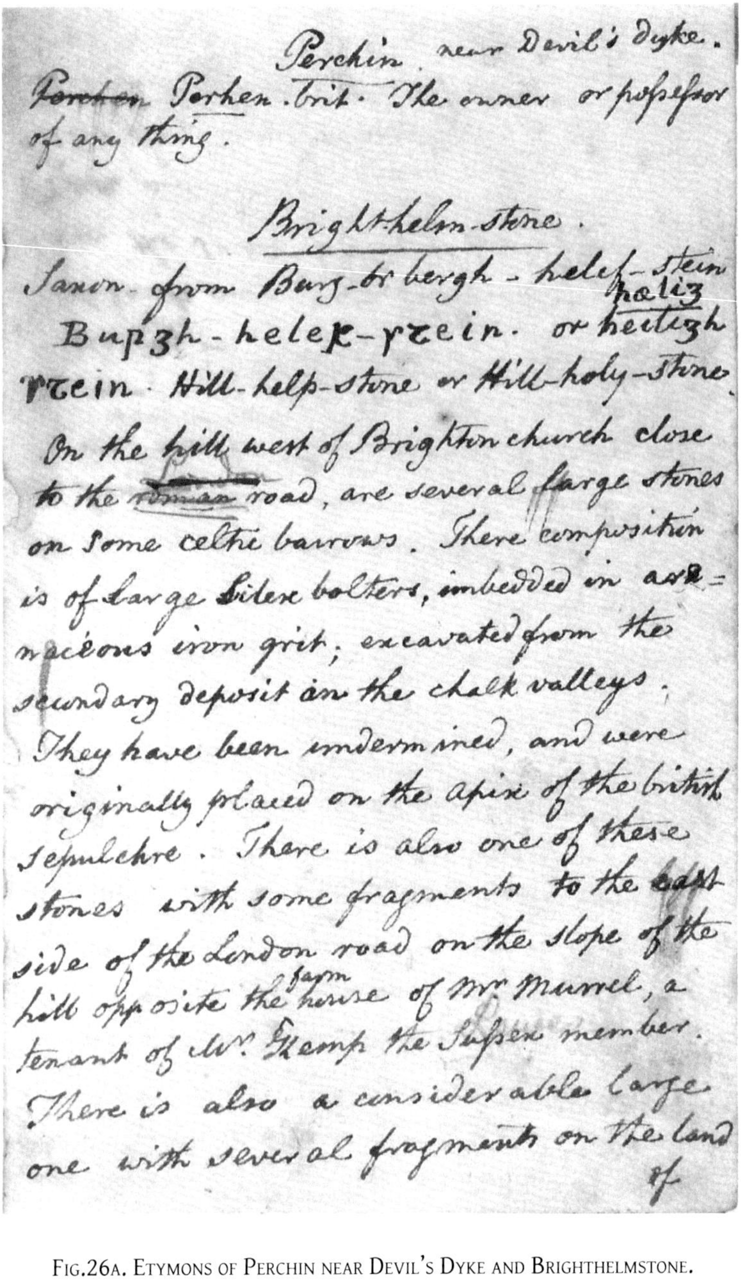

> Perchin. near Devil's dyke.
> ~~Perchen~~ Perhen. brit. The owner or possessor of any thing.
>
> Brighthelm-stone.
> Saxon. from Burg-or bergh - helef-stein
> Bupʒh - heleʁ - ʃtein. or heiligh
> ʃtein. Hill-help-stone or Hill-holy-stone.
> On the hill west of Brighton church close to the ~~roman~~ road, are several large stones on some celtic barrows. There composition is of large silex bolters, imbedded in are-naceous iron grit; excavated from the secundary deposit in the chalk valleys. They have been undermined, and were originally placed on the apix of the british sepulchre. There is also one of these stones with some fragments to the east side of the London road on the slope of the hill opposite the farm house of Mr. Murrel, a tenant of Mr. Kemp the Sussex member. There is also a considerable large one with several fragments on the land of

FIG.26A. ETYMONS OF PERCHIN NEAR DEVIL'S DYKE AND BRIGHTHELMSTONE.

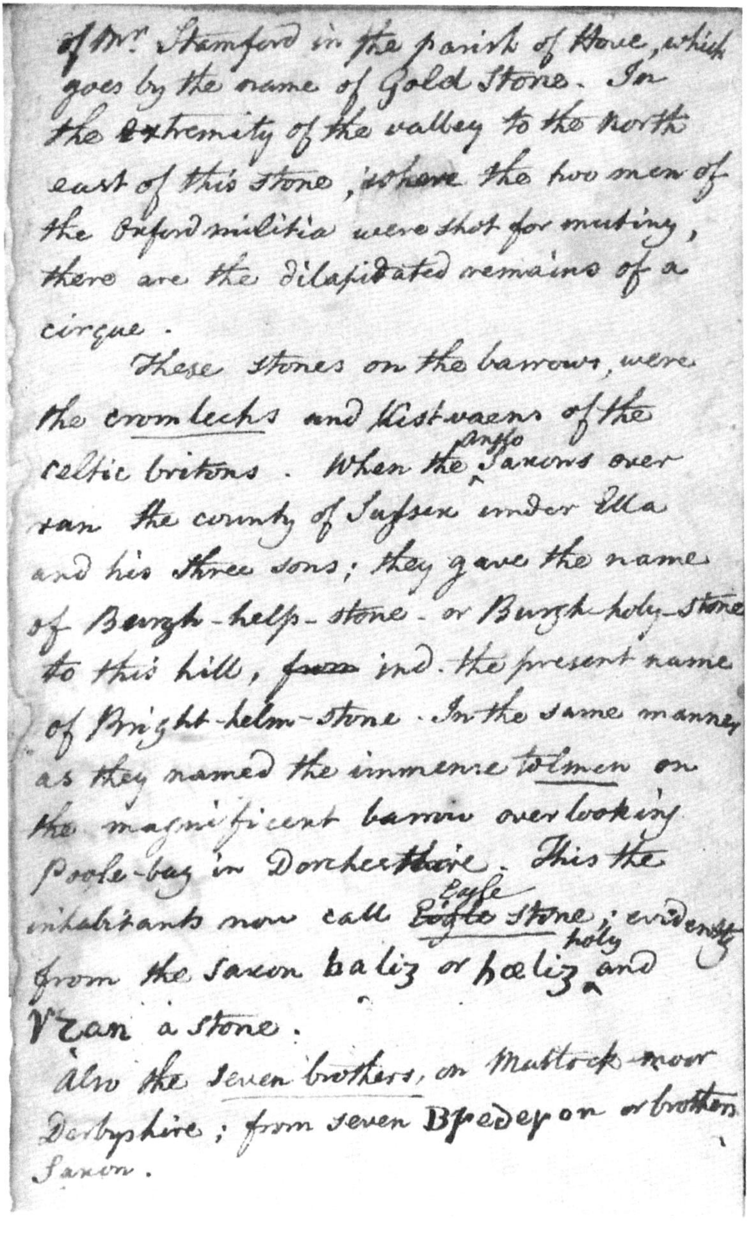

of Mr. Stamford in the parish of Hove, which goes by the name of Gold Stone. In the extremity of the valley to the north east of this stone, where the two men of the Oxford militia were shot for muting, there are the dilapidated remains of a cirque.

These stones on the barrows, were the cromlechs and kistvaens of the celtic britons. When the Saxons over ran the county of Sussex under Ella and his three sons; they gave the name of Beurgh-help-stone - or Beurgh-holy-Stone to this hill, from ind. the present name of Bright-helm-stone. In the same manner as they named the immense tolmen on the magnificent barrow overlooking Poole-bay in Dorsetshire. This the inhabitants now call Eagle Stone; evidently from the saxon ha liz or hœliz holy, and Υʒan a stone.

Also the seven brothers, on Mattock moor Darbyshire; from seven Bpeðeɲ on or brothers Saxon.

FIG. 26B. ETYMONS OF PERCHIN NEAR DEVIL'S DYKE AND BRIGHTHELMSTONE.

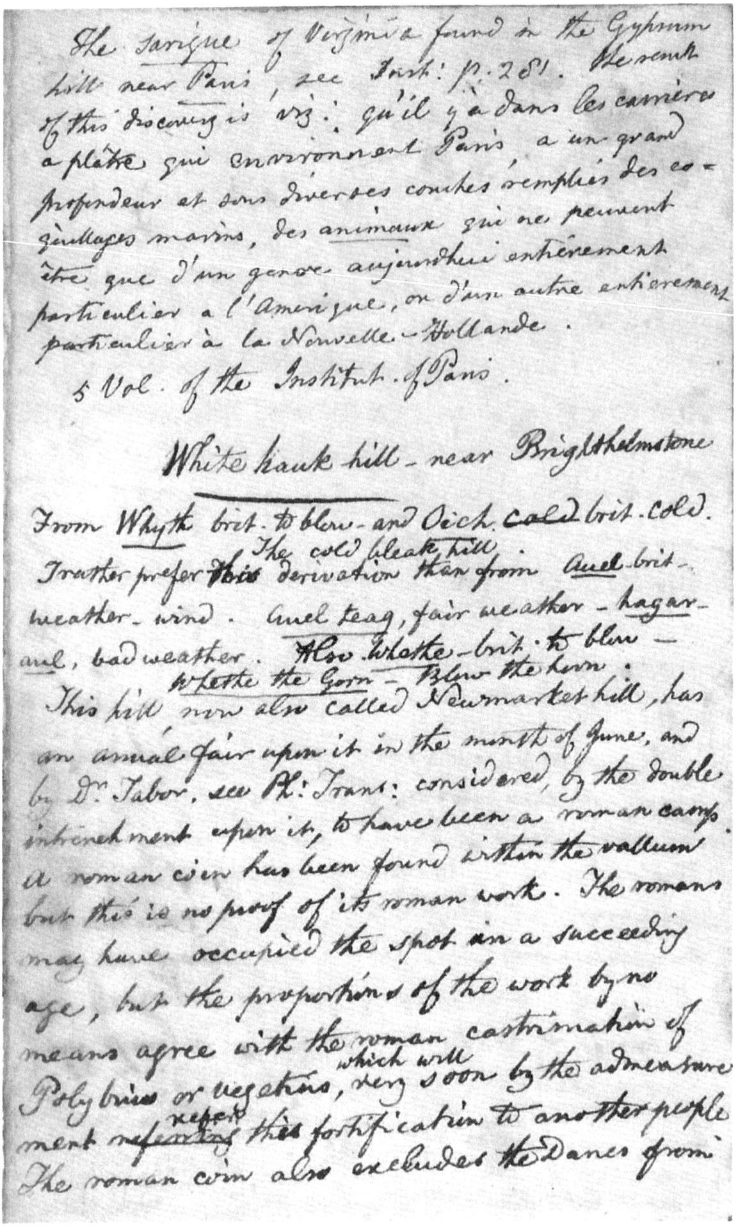

The sarigue of Virginia found in the Gypsum
hill near Paris, see Insti: p. 281. The result
of this discovery is viz: qu'il y a dans les carrières
a plâtre qui environnent Paris, a un grand
profondeur et sous diverses couches remplies des coquillages marins, des animaux qui ne peuvent
être que d'un genre aujourd'hui entièrement
particulier a l'Amerique, ou d'un autre entièrement
particulier à la Nouvelle-Hollande.
5 Vol. of the Institut. of Paris.

White hawk hill – near Brighthelmstone

From Whyth brit. to blow – and Oich. cold brit. cold.
I rather prefer ~~this~~ The cold bleak hill derivation than from Auel brit.
weather – wind. Auel teag, fair weather – hagar-
auel, bad weather. Also Whethe – brit. to blow –
Whethe the Gorn – Blow the horn.
This hill now also called Newmarket hill, has
an annual fair upon it in the month of June, and
by Dr. Tabor, see Ph: Trans: considered, by the double
intrenchment upon it, to have been a roman camp.
A roman coin has been found within the vallum
but this is no proof of its roman work. The romans
may have occupied the spot in a succeeding
age, but the proportions of the work by no
means agree with the roman castrimation of
Polybius or Vegetius, which will very soon by the admeasure
ment ~~referring~~ refer this fortification to another people
The roman coin also excludes the Danes from

Fig.27a. Etymons of Whitehawk hill near Brighthelmstone, Preston, Broil near Ringmeer, Blatchington, With-dean and Liddshill – Preston.

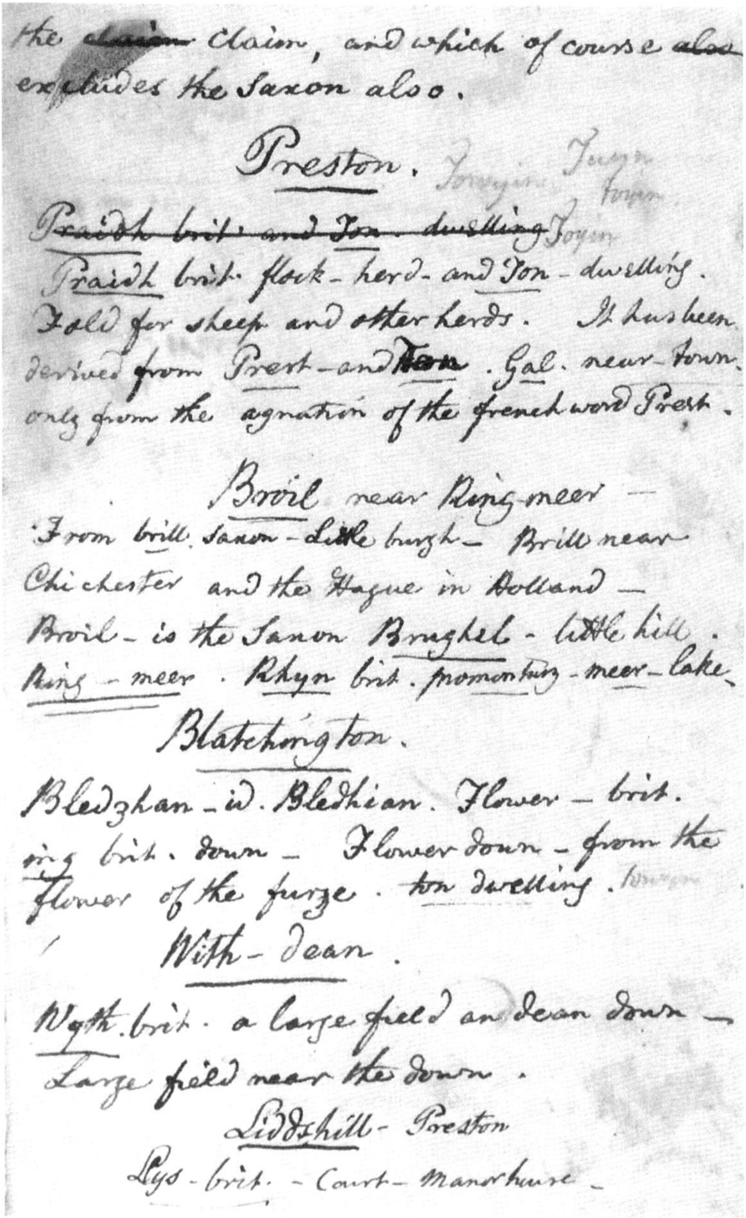
the ~~claim~~ Claim, and which of course also
excludes the Saxon also.
Preston.
~~Praidh brit and Ton dwelling~~
Praidh brit. flock-herd- and Ton - dwelling.
Fold for sheep and other herds. It has been
derived from Prest-and ~~Ton~~. Gal. near-town.
only from the agnation of the french word Prest.
Broil near Ring-meer -
From brill. Saxon - little burgh - Brill near
Chichester and the Hague in Holland -
Broil - is the Saxon Brughel - little hill.
Ring - meer. Rhyn brit. promontory - meer - lake.
Blatchington.
Bledzhan - id. Bledhian. Flower - brit.
ing brit. down - Flower down - from the
flower of the furze. ton dwelling.
With - dean.
Wyth. brit. a large field an dean down -
Large field near the down.
Liddshill - Preston
Llys - brit. - Court - Manor house -

Fig.27b. Etymons of Whitehawk hill near Brighthelmstone, Preston, Broil near Ringmeer, Blatchington, With-dean and Liddshill – Preston.

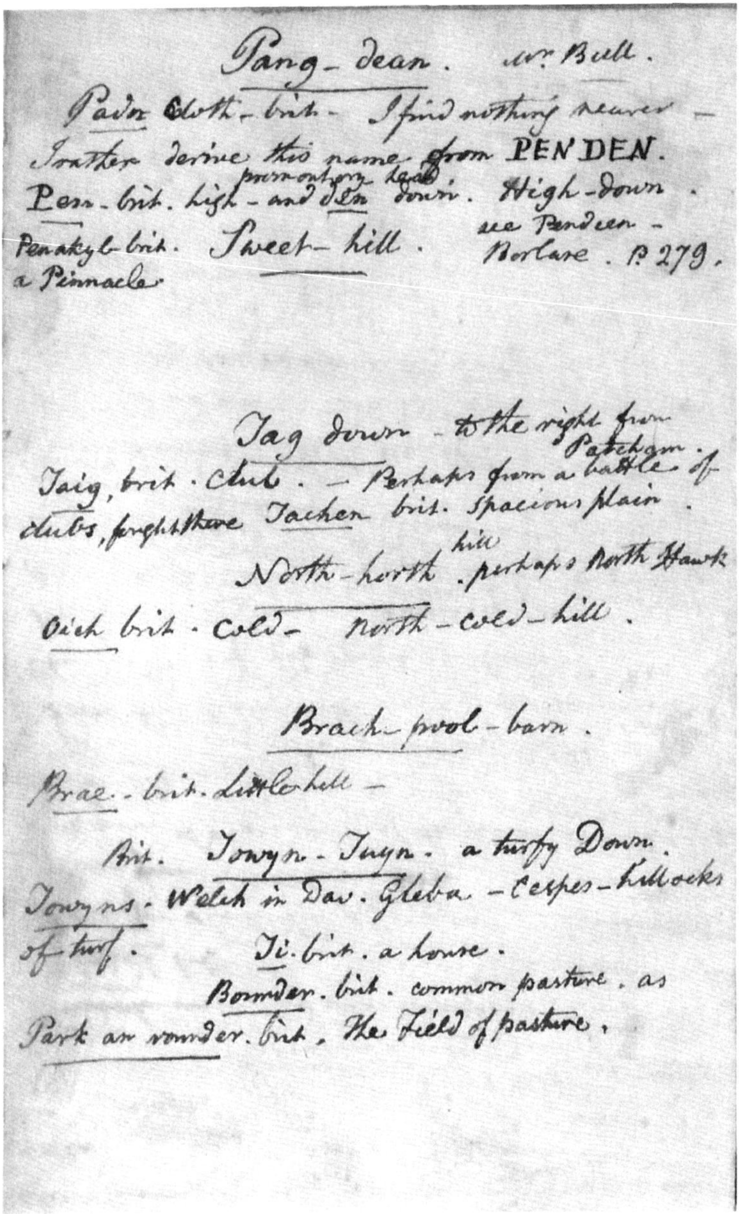
Pang-dean. Mr. Bell.
Pador Cloth-brit. I find nothing nearer —
I rather derive this name from PENDEN.
Pen-brit. high — and Den down. promontory head. High-down.
Penakyl-brit. Sweet-hill. see Pendeen —
a Pinnacle. Borlase. P. 279.

Tag down — to the right from Patcham.
Taig, brit. club. — Perhaps from a battle of
clubs, fought there Tachen brit. spacious plain.
North-horth hill. perhaps North Hawk
Oich brit. cold — North-cold-hill.

Brach-pool-barn.
Brae-brit. Little hill —
Brit. Towyn-Tuyn. a turfy Down.
Towyns. Welch in Dav. Gleba — Cespes — hillocks
of turf. Ti. brit. a house.
Bounder. brit. common pasture. as
Park an vounder. brit. the Field of pasture.

Fig.28a. Etymons of Pang-dean, Tag down, North-horsh hill, Brach-pool-barn, various hills near Preston, Poynings, Lewes, Glyne, Radmil and Uckfield.

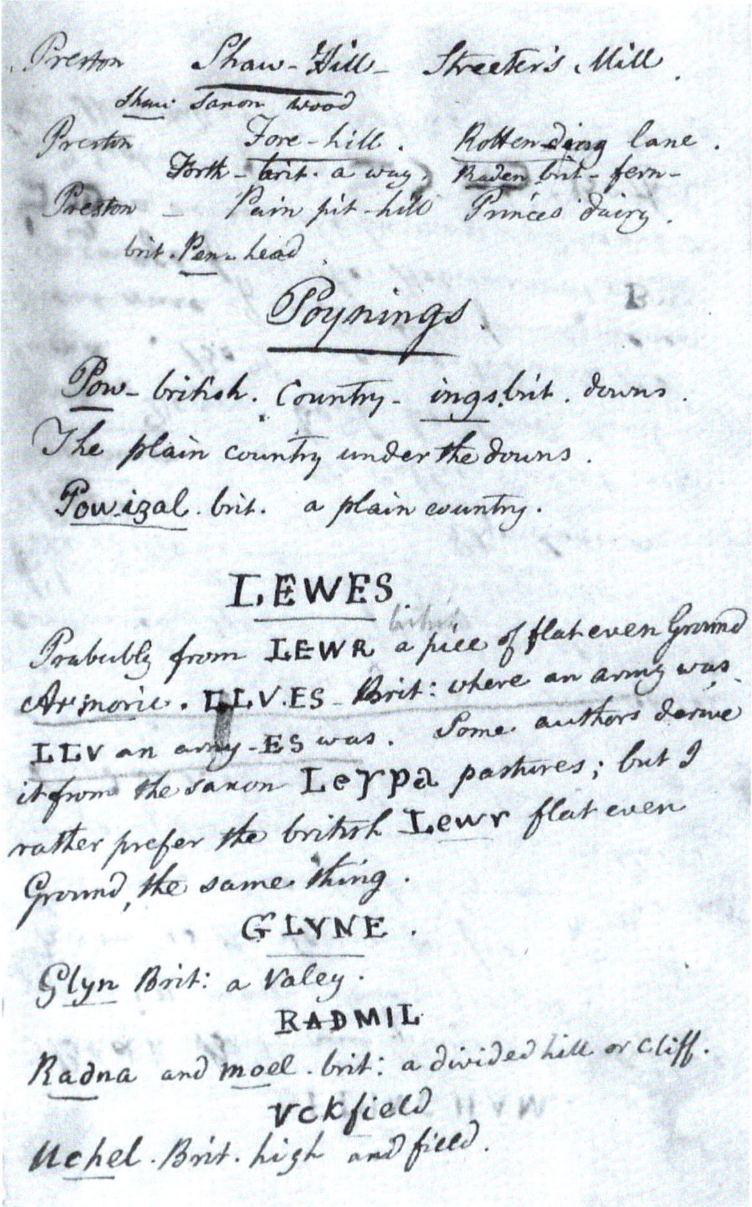

> Preston   Shaw-Hill_ Streeter's Mill.
>   Shaw Saxon wood
> Preston   Fore-Hill.   Rottendean lane.
>   Forth-brit. a way, Braden brit.-fern-
> Preston _   Pain pit-hill Princes dairy.
>   brit.Penn head.
>
> ## Poynings.
>
> Pow-british. Country_ ings.brit. downs.
> The plain country under the downs.
> Powizal. brit. a plain country.
>
> ## LEWES
>
> Probably from LEWR british a piece of flat even Ground
> Armorie. LLVES Brit: where an army was.
> LLV an army -ES was. Some authors derive
> it from the saxon Leypa pastures; but I
> rather prefer the british Lewr flat even
> Ground, the same thing.
>
> ## GLYNE.
>
> Glyn Brit: a Valey.
>
> ## RADMIL
>
> Radna and moel. brit: a divided hill or cliff.
>
> ## Vckfield
>
> Uchel. Brit. high and field.

FIG. 28B. ETYMONS OF PANG-DEAN, TAG DOWN, NORTH-HORSH HILL, BRACH-POOL-BARN, VARIOUS HILLS NEAR PRESTON, POYNINGS, LEWES, GLYNE, RADMIL AND UCKFIELD.

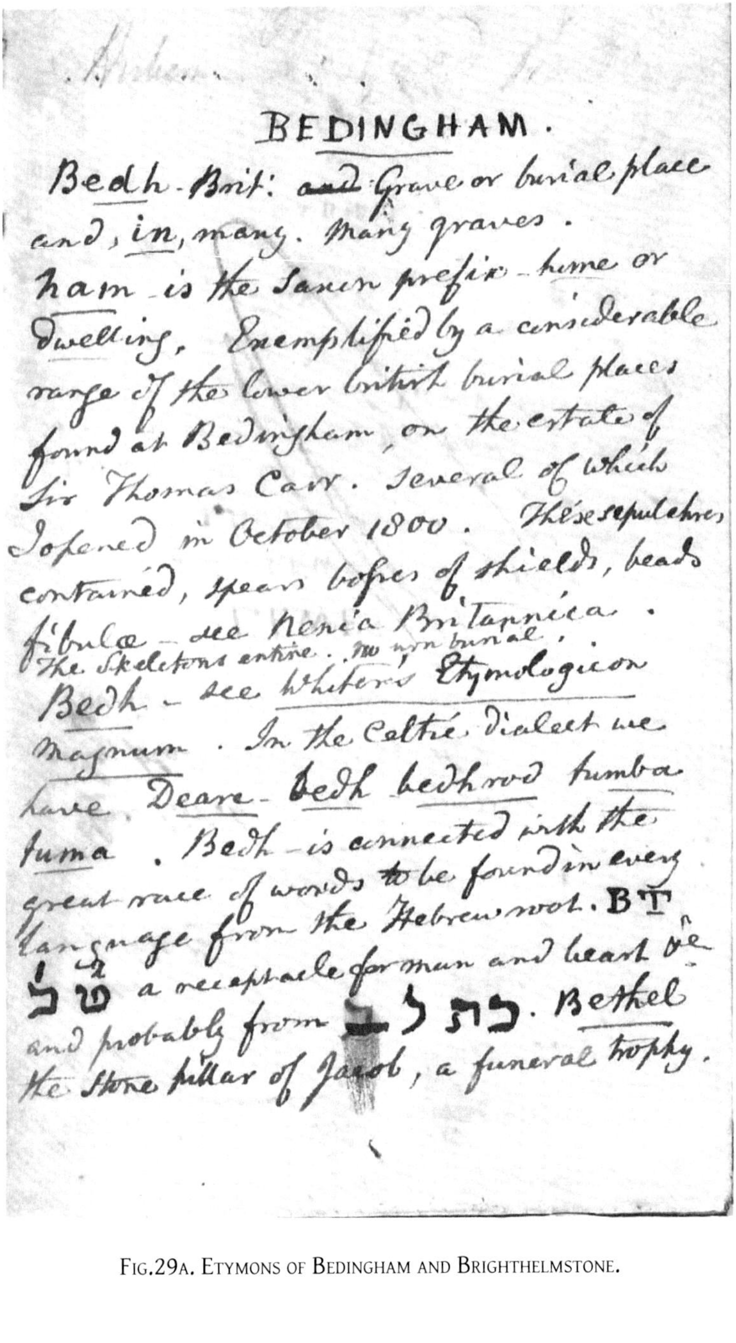

BEDINGHAM.

Bedh - Brit: ~~and~~ Grave or burial place and, in, many. Many graves. ham is the Saxon prefix - home or Dwelling. Exemplified by a considerable range of the lower British burial places found at Bedingham, on the estate of Sir Thomas Carr. Several of which I opened in October 1800. These sepulchres contained, spear bosses of shields, beads fibulæ — see Nenia Britannica. The Skeletons entire.. no urn burial. Bedh — see Whiter's Etymologicon Magnum. In the Celtic dialect we have Deare — bedh bedhrod tumba tuma. Bedh — is connected with the great race of words to be found in every language from the Hebrew root. בּת a receptacle for man and beast בּע and probably from בּיתּ־אל Bethel the Stone pillar of Jacob, a funeral trophy.

FIG. 29A. ETYMONS OF BEDINGHAM AND BRIGHTHELMSTONE.

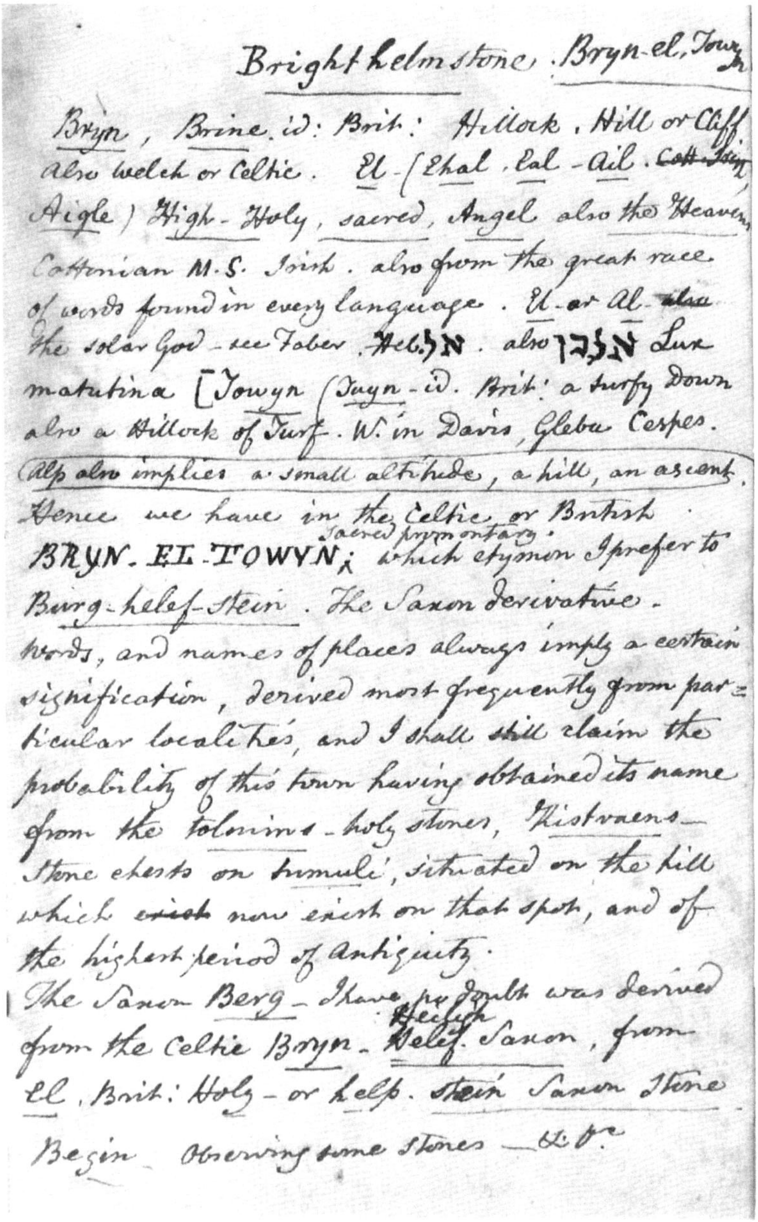

4. Sussex Placename derivations and miscellania

> Brighthelmstone. Bryn-el, Towyn
>
> Bryn, Brine. id: Brit: Hillock. Hill or Cliff
> also Welch or Celtic. El - (Ehal. Eal - Ail. Cott Hey
> Aigle) High - Holy, sacred, Angel also the Heaven
> Cottonian M.S. Irish. also from the great race
> of words found in every language. El - or Al - also
> the solar God - see Faber. Heb. אֵל. also אוֹרָה Lux
> matutina [Towyn (Tuyn - id. Brit: a turfy down
> also a Hillock of Turf. W. in Davis, Gleba Cespes.
> Alp also implies a small altitude, a hill, an ascent.
> Hence we have in the Celtic or British
>   sacred promontory.
> BRYN. EL. TOWYN; which etymon I prefer to
> Burg-helef-Stein. The Saxon derivative -
> Words, and names of places always imply a certain
> signification, derived most frequently from par-
> ticular localities, and I shall still claim the
> probability of this town having obtained its name
> from the tolmins - holy stones, Kistvaens -
> Stone chests on tumuli, situated on the hill
> which exist now exist on that spot, and of
> the highest period of antiquity.
> The Saxon Berg - I have no doubt was derived
> from the Celtic Bryn - Helef Saxon, from
> El, Brit: Holy - or help. Stein Saxon Stone
> Begin - Observing some stones — &c.

FIG. 29B. ETYMONS OF BEDINGHAM AND BRIGHTHELMSTONE.

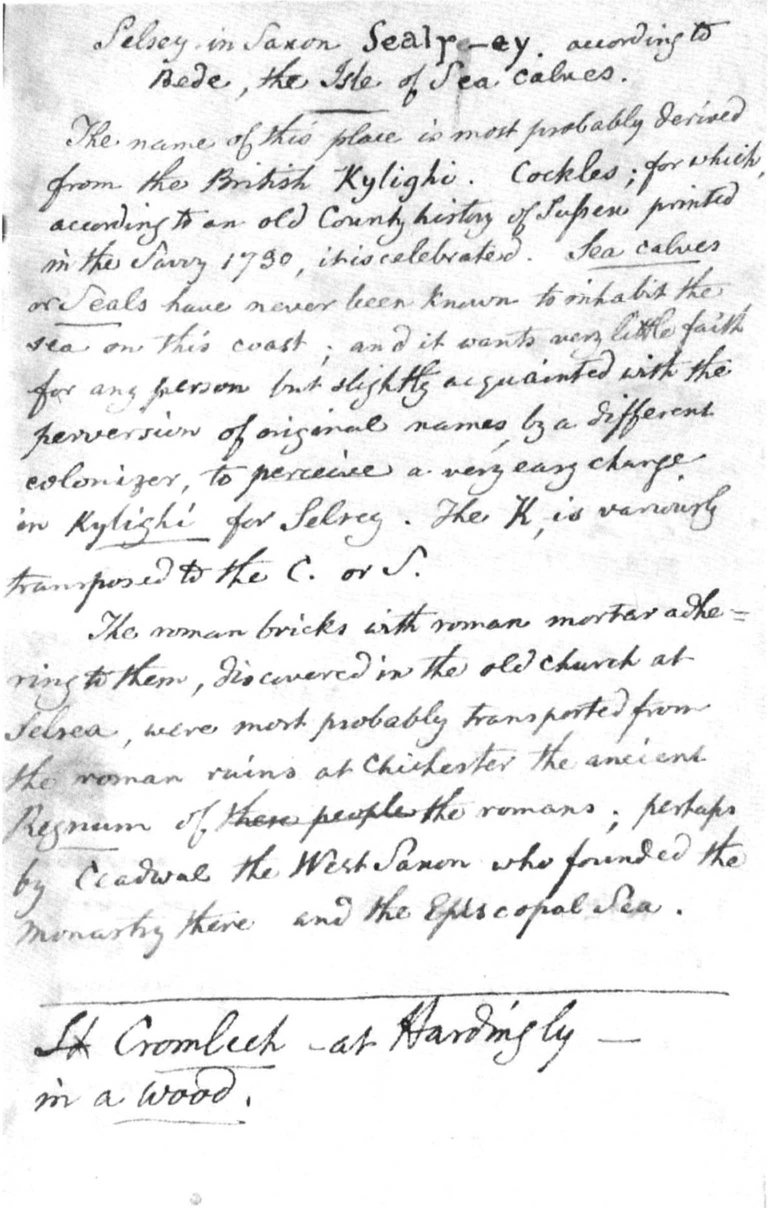

> Selsey in Saxon Sealp—ey, according to Bede, the Isle of Sea calves.
>
> The name of this place is most probably derived from the British Kylighi. Cockles; for which, according to an old County history of Sussex printed in the Savoy 1730, it is celebrated. Sea calves or Seals have never been known to inhabit the sea on this coast; and it wants very little faith for any person but slightly acquainted with the perversion of original names by a different colonizer, to perceive a very easy change in Kylighi for Selsey. The K is variously transposed to the C. or S.
>
> The roman bricks with roman mortar adhering to them, discovered in the old church at Selsea, were most probably transported from the roman ruins at Chichester the ancient Regnum of these people the romans; perhaps by Ceadwal the West Saxon who founded the monastry there and the Episcopal Sea.
>
> A Cromlech at Hardingly — in a Wood.

FIG.30. ETYMON OF SELSEY, WITH TERSE REFERENCE TO A CROMLECH IN A WOOD AT ARDINGLY.

5. Epilogue

During the Reverend Skinner's visit to Brighton in 1821 after James Douglas's death he went for a short walk to the north-west of Hollingbury camp and came upon *'two persons at a distance appearing employed in digging into a tumulus, I walked up to them and found it to be as I imagined; their operation being directed against a flat barrow, twenty or twenty five feet in diameter, from which they were taking the large flints for building. On inquiring I found they had yesterday met with a large clay urn (containing ashes) which the man broke with his pick axe. On examining the fragments, I perceived it was exactly similar to what I have so frequently met with in Wiltshire and Somersetshire – rude unbaked clay, ornamented with lines marked on the surface: The man informed me he had dug up several of the same kind, when working for Mr Douglas. He moreover informed me that several of these urns had been thrown away, at the house he occupied at Preston; after his decease by his successor on the premises: such is the fate of our pursuit – laughed at and ridiculed whilst we live, and our labours consigned to be trampled under feet after we are gone'* (BM ADD MS 33658).

Bibliography

Bell, M. 1977 *Excavations at Bishopstone*, Sussex Archaeol Collect 115.

Curwen, E., Curwen,E.C. 1920 'The earthworks of Rewell Hill, near Arundel', *Sussex Archaeol Collect* 61, 20-30.

Douglas, J. 1785 *A Dissertation on the Antiquity of the Earth*

Douglas, J. 1793 *Nenia Britannica or, A Sepulchral History of Great Britain from the earliest period to the General Conversion to Christianity*. London

Douglas, J. 1818 'On the Ancient barrows observable on the South Downs', *Provincial Magazine* Vol.1, No.1, August 1818.

Grinsell, L.V. 1934 'Sussex Barrows', *Sussex Archaeol Collect* 75, p.217-275.

Haydon, B.R.,1853 *Life of Haydon*, Vol 3.

Hills, C., Penn, K., Rickett, R. 1984 *The Anglo-Saxon Cemetery at Spong Hill, North Elmham Part III: Catalogue of Inhumations*, East Anglian Archaeology Report No.21.

King, T. 1845 *Archaeological Journal* Vol II, 80

Jessup, R. 1976 *Man of many talents. An Informal Biography of James Douglas 1753-1819*, Phillimore.

Lyne, M.A.B. 1995 'The Hassocks cemetery', *Sussex Archaeol Collect* 132 (1994), p.53-85.

Longworth, I.H. 1984 *Collared Urns of the Bronze Age in Great Britain and Ireland*, C.U.P.

MacGregor, A., Bolick, E. 1993 *Ashmolean Museum Oxford. A Summary Catalogue of the Anglo-Saxon Collections (Non-Ferrous Metals),* BAR Brit Ser 230.

McOmish, D., Hayden, G. 2015 'Survey and excavation at Goblestubbs Copse, Arundel, West Sussex', *Sussex Archaeol Collect* 153, 1-28.

Sicklemore, R. 1827 *History of Brighton and its environs, from the earliest period to the present time*. 5th Edition.

Toms, H.S. 1927 'Sarsens in Sussex', *The Sussex County Magazine* Vol 1, No.12, 530-33